THE YEAR YC
WERE BORN

GW00374783

1961

A fascinating book about the year 1961 with information on:
Events of the year UK, Adverts of 1961, Cost of living, Births, Deaths, Sporting events,
Book publications, Movies, Music, World events and People in power.

INDEX

uary

st The Betting and Gaming Act 1960 was a British Act of Parliament that legalised additional forms of gambling in the United Kingdom. It was passed on the 1st September 1960 and came into effect on the 1st January 1961.

The farthing coin used since the thirteenth century ceases to be legal tender in the United Kingdom.

The British farthing (1/4d) coin was a unit of currency of one quarter of a penny, or 1/960 of a pound sterling. It was minted in bronze, and replaced the earlier copper farthings. It was used during the reign of six monarchs: Victoria, Edward VII, George V, Edward VIII, George VI and Elizabeth II, ceasing to be legal tender from the 1st January 1961. It featured two different designs on its reverse during its 100 years in circulation: from 1860 until 1936, the image of Britannia; and from 1937 onwards, the image of a wren. Like all British coinage, it bore the portrait of the monarch on the obverse.

d The Conservative Monday Club (usually known as the Monday Club) is a British political pressure group, aligned with the Conservative Party, though no longer endorsed by it. It also has links to the Democratic Unionist Party (DUP) and Ulster Unionist Party (UUP) in Northern Ireland. Founded in 1961, in the belief that the Macmillan ministry had taken the party too far to the left, the club became embroiled in the decolonisation and immigration debate, inevitably highlighting the controversial issue of race, which has dominated its image ever since. The club was known for its fierce opposition to non-White immigration to Britain and its support for apartheid-era South Africa and Rhodesia. By 1971, the club had 35 MPs, six of them ministers, and 35 peers, with membership (including branches) totalling about 10,000.

Members of the Soviet Portland Spy Ring are arrested in London. The Portland Spy Ring was a Soviet spy ring that operated in England from the late 1950s until 1961, when the core of the network was arrested by the British security services. It is one of the most famous examples of the use of illegal residents—spies who operate in a foreign country but without the cover of their embassy. Its members included Harry Houghton, Ethel Gee, Gordon Lonsdale and Morris and Lona Cohen (also known as Peter and Helen Kroger).

January

7th | The Avengers is a British espionage television series created in 1961. It initially focused on Dr. David Kee (Ian Hendry), aided by John Steed (Patrick Macnee). Hendry left after the first series; Steed then becam the main character, partnered with a succession of assistants. His most famous assistants were intellige stylish and assertive women: Cathy Gale (Honor Blackman), Emma Peel (Diana Rigg) and Tara King (Lind Thorson). The series ran from 1961 until 1969, screening as one-hour episodes for its entire run. The pi episode, "Hot Snow", aired on the 7th January 1961.

The final episode, "Bizarre", aired on the 21st April 1969 in the United States, and on the 21st May 1969 the United Kingdom. The Avengers was produced by ABC Television, a contractor within the ITV networ

After a merger with Rediffusion London in July 1968, ABC Television became Thames Television, which continued production of the series, though it was still broadcast under the ABC name. By 1969, The Avengers was shown in more than 90 countries. ITV produced a sequel series, The New Avengers (1976 1977), with Patrick Macnee returning as John Steed, and two new partners.

February

5th | The Sunday Telegraph is a British broadsheet newspaper. It was founded on the 5th February 1961 and published by the Telegraph Media Group, a division of Press Holdings. It is the sister paper of The Daily Telegraph, also published by the Telegraph Media Group. The Sunday Telegraph was originally a separa operation with a different editorial staff, but since 2013 the Telegraph has been a seven-day operation

15th | The United Kingdom held a national pre-selection to choose the song that would go to the 1961 Eurov Song Contest. It was held on the 15th February 1961 and presented by Katie Boyle. The songs were vot on by a total of 120 jurors aged between 19 and 40.

19th |

Police break up a demonstration outside the Belgian embassy in London, protesting about the murder the ex-Congolese Prime Minister, Patrice Lumumba.

Holy Loch becomes the United States Navy's FBM Refit Site One and home base to its Submarine Squadron 14 (equipped with Polaris nuclear missiles) with the arrival of tender USS Proteus.

INS Vikrant (R11) is commissioned as the Indian Navy's first aircraft carrier in Belfast, having been completed here by Harland and Wolff.

Edwin Bush (1940–1961) was the first criminal in Britain to be caught through the use of the Identikit facial composite system. He was 21 years old when he was executed at Pentonville Prison in London on the 6th July 1961. Edwin Bush was sentenced to death on the 12th May 1961 at the Old Bailey, for the capital murder on the 3rd March 1961 of Elsie May Batten, a 59-year-old assistant in an antique shop in Cecil Court off Charing Cross Road in London. Mrs Batten had been found stabbed to death with an antique dagger in the shop where she worked. Edwin Bush was the second to last criminal executed in London and the twelfth to last in the United Kingdom.

"Water towers" speech: The Minister of Health, Enoch Powell, in a speech to a Conservative Party conference, proposes closing down of large, traditional psychiatric hospitals in favour of more community-based care.

The five members of the Portland Spy Ring go on trial at the Old Bailey accused of passing nuclear secrets to the Soviet Union.

Black and white £5 notes cease to be legal tender.

March

21st | Shakespeare Memorial Theatre, Stratford-upon-Avon, becomes the Royal Shakespeare Theatre and its company the Royal Shakespeare Company.

21st | The Beatles perform at the legendary Cavern Club in Liverpool for the first time.

April

3rd | The Jaguar E-Type, a sports car capable of reaching speeds of 150 mph, is launched as a two-seater roadster or 2+2 coupé. The Jaguar E-Type is a British sports car that was manufactured by Jaguar Cars L between 1961 and 1975. Its combination of beauty, high performance, and competitive pricing establis the model as an icon of the motoring world. The E-Type's claimed 150 mph (241 km/h) top speed, sub-second 0 to 60 mph (97 km/h) acceleration, monocoque construction, disc brakes, rack-and-pinion steering, and independent front and rear suspension distinguished the car and spurred industry-wide changes.

Tottenham Hotspur wins the Football League First Division for the second time, with a 2–1 win over Sheffield Wednesday. They have not won the contest since.

Sierra Leone gains independence from the UK.

The Top Storey Club was a nightclub in Bolton, Greater Manchester, UK. It achieved notoriety for a fire which occurred in May 1961 in which 19 people perished. The club was located on Crown Street in Bolton and was on the top floors of an old mill warehouse building. From the street front, the building had three floors but the warehouse was built on a slope so the rear had eight floors looking out on to the River Croal which at this point ran in a brick-lined channel. The club was opened in December 1960 by Stanley Wilcock, who rented the building, using the lower floors for his business, making kitchen furniture. On the night of the fire, the club was quiet with it being a Monday. Between 20 and 25 people were in the club. At 11pm, less than half an hour after the visit by the owner, the manager Bill Bohannon smelt smoke. He went down the single wooden staircase, which was the only means of access and egress. Upon arriving at the ground floor, he saw smoke coming under the door leading to the furniture workshop. He kicked the door down and was confronted with a raging inferno. The intensity of the fire prevented him returning upstairs, but he managed to escape. This inferno quickly spread up the stairs towards the club. As there was no other means of escape, some customers took to jumping from the windows. The windows available were those at the back, where there was an eight-floor drop onto bricks by the river channel.

Betting shops become legal under terms of the Betting and Gaming Act 1960.

The United Kingdom becomes a member of the OECD. Organisation for Economic Co-operation and Development is an intergovernmental economic organisation with 36 member countries, founded in 1961 to stimulate economic progress and world trade. It is a forum of countries describing themselves as committed to democracy and the market economy, providing a platform to compare policy experiences, seek answers to common problems, identify good practices and coordinate domestic and international policies of its members.

Tottenham Hotspur becomes the first English football team this century, and only the third in history, to win the double of the league title and FA Cup, with a 2–0 victory over Leicester City in the FA Cup Final. (The last previous team to achieve this were Aston Villa in 1897)

George Blake is sentenced to 42 years imprisonment for spying, having been found guilty of being a double agent in the pay of the Soviet Union. In 1961, Blake fell under suspicion after revelations by Polish defector Michael Goleniewski and others. He was arrested when he arrived in London after being summoned from Lebanon, where he had been enrolled at the Middle East Centre for Arabic Studies (MECAS). Three days into his interrogation, Blake denied he was tortured or blackmailed by the North Koreans. Without thinking what he was saying, he stated that he had switched sides voluntarily. He then gave his MI6 interrogators a full confession.

Peter Benenson's article "The Forgotten Prisoners" is published in several internationally read newspapers. This will later be thought of as the founding of the human rights organisation Amnesty International.

June

8th Prince Edward, Duke of Kent, marries Katharine Worsley at York Minster. The couple were married by T Most Rev. and Rt Hon. Michael Ramsey, Archbishop of York, in York Minster, the "Westminster Abbey the North," according to the Book of Common Prayer. This was the first royal wedding held in York Min since Edward III married Philippa of Hainault in 1328. His wife converted to Catholicism in 1994. Becaus this conversion occurred after their marriage, it did not because the Duke to lose his place in the line of succession, as the Act of Settlement 1701 only applied where the spouse was a Catholic at the time of marriage. The disqualification by marrying a Catholic was removed by the Succession to the Crown Act 2013. The couple's son, Nicholas, also converted to Catholicism and he is excluded from the line of succession in accordance with the Act of Settlement 1701 which continue to bar Catholics from the thr

14th The Government unveils new "panda" crossings with push button controls for pedestrians, due to concerns about the increasing volume of traffic. The new crossings first appeared on British streets in 1962.

19th The British protectorate ends in Kuwait and it becomes an emirate.

27th Michael Ramsey enthroned as the hundredth Archbishop of Canterbury, in succession to Geoffrey Fish

Kuwait requests help from the UK and British troops are sent.

30th The popular radio comedy programme Hancock's Half Hour is aired for the last time.

July

3rd The Suicide Act 1961 is an Act of the Parliament of the United Kingdom. It decriminalised the act of sui in England and Wales so that those who failed in the attempt to kill themselves would no longer be prosecuted. Before the Suicide Act 1961, it was a crime to commit suicide, and anyone who attempted failed could be prosecuted and imprisoned, while the families of those who succeeded could also potentially be prosecuted.

Barclays open their "No. 1 Computer Centre" in Drummond Street, London, with an EMI mainframe computer, Britain's first bank with an in-house computing centre.

At an all-British women's final to The Championships, Wimbledon in tennis, Angela Mortimer beats Christine Truman.

The 1961 British Grand Prix was a Formula One motor race, held on the 15th July 1961 at the Aintree Circuit, near Liverpool. It was race 5 of 8 in both the 1961 World Championship of Drivers and the 1961 International Cup for Formula One Manufacturers.

The Silver Jubilee Bridge (informally the Runcorn Bridge or Runcorn–Widnes Bridge) crosses the River Mersey and the Manchester Ship Canal at Runcorn Gap between Runcorn and Widnes in Halton, England. It is a through arch bridge with a main arch span of 361 yards (330 m). It was opened on the 21st July 1961 as a replacement for the Widnes-Runcorn Transporter Bridge. In 1975–77 the carriageway was widened, after which the bridge was given its official name in honour of the Queen's Silver Jubilee. It carries the A533 road and a cantilevered footway. The bridge is recorded in the National Heritage List for England as a designated Grade II listed building. The bridge closed for repairs and alterations upon the opening of the new Mersey Gateway Bridge and is due to reopen in 2020.

The Government calls for a voluntary "pay pause" in wage increases (continuing to April 1962).

The Lancashire-set film Whistle Down the Wind, starring Hayley Mills and Alan Bates, opens. Whistle Down the Wind is a 1961 British crime film directed by Bryan Forbes, and adapted by Keith Waterhouse and Willis Hall from the 1959 novel of the same name by Mary Hayley Bell. The film stars her daughter, Hayley Mills, who was nominated for the BAFTA Award for Best British Actress and an Academy Juvenile Award for Walt Disney's Pollyanna (1960).

ust

The UK applies for membership of the EEC. The European Economic Community (EEC) was a regional organisation that aimed to bring about economic integration among its member states. It was created by the Treaty of Rome of 1957. Upon the formation of the European Union (EU) in 1993, the EEC was incorporated and renamed the European Community (EC). In 2009, the EC's institutions were absorbed into the EU's wider framework and the community ceased to exist.

August

16th | The play Lady Chatterley by John Harte – based on D. H. Lawrence's novel – opens at the Arts Theatre in London and is well-reviewed by West End theatre critic, Harold Hobson.

23rd | Police launch a manhunt for the perpetrator of the A6 murder, who shot dead 36-year-old Michael Gregsten and paralysed his mistress Valerie Storie.

25th | Murder of Jacqueline Thomas: Police in Birmingham launch a murder inquiry after the body of a missing teenager is found on an allotment in the Alum Rock area of the city. Jacqueline Mary Thomas was an English 15-year-old biscuit factory worker from Alum Rock, Birmingham, who was sexually assaulted and strangled after disappearing on the 18th August 1961. Her body was discovered a week later close to her home, and the murder sparked a manhunt involving several hundred police officers. A suspect was identified at the time, but there was insufficient evidence to charge him, and the crime remained unsolved for over four decades until a cold case review in the 2000s. In 2007, 70-year-old Anthony Hall – already serving a life sentence for the murder of another teenager – was charged with Thomas's murder. However, a judge subsequently ruled the charge should be stayed owing to the length of time that had passed since the incident. Hall subsequently died in prison.

31st | Premiere of the film Victim, notable as the first in English to use the word "homosexual".

September

1st | First Mothercare shop opens, as Mother-and-Child Centre in Kingston upon Thames. The company was founded by Selim Zilkha and Sir James Goldsmith on the 1st September 1961. It was first listed on the London Stock Exchange in 1972. In May 2018, it was confirmed that Mothercare would close 60 stores in the United Kingdom under company voluntary arrangement schemes affecting three subsidiaries: Mothercare UK Limited, Early Learning Centre Limited and Children's World Limited. The Early Learning Centre business – which operated in 80 UK stores and 400 overseas franchises – was sold to the Entertainer group in March 2019. During the 2019 financial year, the company's Watford headquarters was sold in a leaseback transaction which raised £14.5M. In July 2019, the company said it was planning to spin off its UK retail business due to decreased sales. The company reported that UK store sales fell down by 23.2%, while online sales in the UK were down by 12.1%. The company recorded a worldwide sales drop of 9.4%. In November 2019, the company put Mothercare UK (and Mothercare Business Services) into administration. This means all the UK shops and the UK website will close soon. Mothercare International still trades profitably.

4th | James Pitman's Initial Teaching Alphabet is tested in a number of schools.

14th | Film A Taste of Honey, including themes of interracial relationship, unmarried pregnancy and homosexuality, is released.

15th | Myra Hess gives her last public concert, at London's Royal Festival Hall.

16th | Three people die and 35 are injured when a stand collapses during a Glasgow Rangers football match at Ibrox Park.

17th | Police arrest over 1,300 protesters in Trafalgar Square during a CND rally.

st Religious programme Songs of Praise first broadcast on BBC Television; it will still be running fifty years later. Songs of Praise is a BBC Television religious programme that presents Christian hymns sung in churches of varying denominations from around the UK.

nd Acker Bilk's Stranger on the Shore released. "Stranger on the Shore" is a piece for clarinet written by Acker Bilk for his young daughter and originally named "Jenny" after her. It was subsequently used as the theme tune of a BBC TV drama serial for young people, Stranger on the Shore. It was first released in 1961 in the UK, and then in the US, and reached number 1 in the US and number 2 in the UK.

Points of View, featuring the letters of viewers offering praise, criticism and comments on the television of recent weeks, debuts on BBC Television. The series will still be on the air more than 50 years later.

th Skelmersdale, a small Lancashire town fifteen miles north-east of Liverpool, is designated as a new town and its population will expand over the coming years, bolstered by large council housing developments to rehouse families from inner city slums on Merseyside.

th A volcanic eruption on the South Atlantic British overseas territory of Tristan da Cunha causes the island's entire population to be evacuated to Surrey, where they will remain until 1963.

th Former school friends Mick Jagger and Keith Richards, later of The Rolling Stones, meet each other again by chance on Dartford railway station on the way to their respective colleges and discover their mutual taste for rock and roll.

Mick Jagger

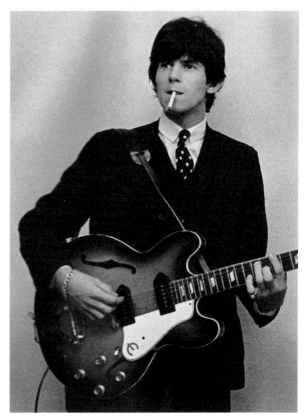

Keith Richards

October

25th | Private Eye is a British fortnightly satirical and current affairs news magazine, founded on the 25th Octob 1961. It is published in London and has been edited by Ian Hislop since 1986. The publication is widely recognised for its prominent criticism and lampooning of public figures. It is also known for its in-depth investigative journalism into under-reported scandals and cover-ups. Private Eye is Britain's best-selling current affairs magazine, and such is its long-term popularity and impact that many of its recurring in-jo have entered popular culture. The magazine bucks the trend of declining circulation for print media, having recorded its highest ever circulation in the second half of 2016. It is privately owned and highly profitable.

November

8th | In a referendum on Sunday opening of public houses in Wales, the counties of Anglesey, Cardiganshire, Caernarfonshire, Carmarthenshire, Denbighshire, Merionethshire, Montgomeryshire and Pembrokeshir all vote to stay "dry", that is, opposed to the Sunday sale of alcohol.

9th | At the Lyceum Theatre, London, Miss United Kingdom, Welsh-born Rosemarie Frankland, becomes the first British winner of the Miss World beauty pageant.

27th | The RAF participates in air drops of food to flood victims in Somalia.

December

4th | Birth control pills become available on the NHS after their availability is backed by Health Minister Enoc Powell.

9th | Tanganyika gains independence from the United Kingdom. Tanganyika was a sovereign state, comprisir the mainland part of present-day Tanzania that existed from 1961 until 1964. It first gained independer from the United Kingdom on 9 December 1961 as a state headed by Queen Elizabeth II before becomir republic within the Commonwealth of Nations a year later. After signing the Articles of Union on 22 Ap 1964 and passing an Act of Union on 25 April, Tanganyika officially joined with the People's Republic of Zanzibar and Pemba to form the United Republic of Tanganyika and Zanzibar on Union Day, 26 April 19 The new state changed its name to the United Republic of Tanzania within a year.

The Beatles play their first gig in the south of England, at Aldershot. Due to an advertising failure, only people turn up. In the early hours of the following morning they play an impromptu set at a London clu

15th | The BBC broadcasts the first Comedy Playhouse. The series broadcasts a series of one-off unrelated sitcoms. Over the next 14 years the series would air the pilot episodes of many popular comedies, including Steptoe and Son, Till Death Us Do Part, Up Pompeii!, The Liver Birds, Are You Being Served? / Last of the Summer Wine.

20,270,000 PEOPLE

will read
RADIO TIMES
with
advertising for
SOBELL

Are you missing potential profits? During the nine days' life of Radio Times over *twenty million* people will see the issues carrying the powerful advertising for the exciting 19" "Luxury Landscape" Sobell T.V. (T280).

People making major buying decisions make them in the comfortable, relaxed atmosphere of their own homes. Advertising in Radio Times is seen not once, but many times, for Radio Times is read again and again.

See how your sales improve when you stock goods advertised in Radio Times—Britain's most read magazine.

More
people buy
goods
advertised
in

Radio Times

Britain's
most-read magazine

T120/R 650cc o.h.v.

1961 TRIUMPH
Bonneville 120

Absolute ultimate in performance, and handling qualities—everything a knowledgeable sportsman desires in a high performance road-sports motorcycle. The famous dual carburetor, 50 horsepower "Bonneville" holds the American speed record for standard production motorcycles at 147 mph, set in September, 1959—it's the most sought after motorcycle available today!

The dual carburetor competition "C" model Bonneville incorporates certain alterations from standard specification which make it especially suitable for cross-country sporting events, or for use over difficult terrain. The exhaust system is of the dual upswept variety to add ground clearance; the crankcase is protected by a special metal shield, and the tires are ideal for use over extremely rough roads or trails. Full lighting equipment, plus all of the other Bonneville standard accessories (except tachometer) makes the "C" Bonneville an all-around, unusually high performance motorcycle, designed particularly for the experienced sportsman who will appreciate the special features of this model.

Can't beat the new cross-country steering geometry, plus the Bonneville engine — a winning combination!

T120/C 650cc o.h.v.

See reverse side for technical specifications

This camera inspires

CONFIDENCE

You feel right at home with this camera as soon as you pick it up. The well-designed body sits lightly and easily in your hand. The lens is completely self-erecting—the camera opens by pressing a small button on the side. Thus, in one simple movement the camera is ready for work. The direct-vision view-finder enables you to see your picture easily and clearly, before you take it. The body shutter release, too, fitted on all models over £4 10 0, is in just the right position for you to operate it. You will find this camera a real pleasure to handle, and it is Made in England, of course.

Ensign

SELFIX 220

The Selfix 220 takes 12 pictures size $2\frac{1}{4} \times 2\frac{1}{4}$ in., or 16 pictures $2\frac{1}{4} \times 1\frac{5}{8}$ in. on size E.20 film. A mask is provided to give the correct vision for the smaller picture—a mechanical exposure counting device is incorporated which enables you to dispense with the ruby window.

S/220/4P, *Ensar Anast.* f/4.5, *Prontor II* shutter

£6 10 0

Other models from **£3 5 0** to **£10 17 6**

ENSIGN Ltd. · HIGH HOLBORN · LONDON, W.C.I

EXCITING PICTURE STORIES THAT THRILL — IN A PAPER EVERY BOY WILL ENJOY!

THE VICTOR

EVERY MONDAY

Price 4½d

No. 12
MAY 13th
1961

SEPHTON STAYED AT HIS POST!

In May 1941, the British hospital ship Aba was attacked in the Mediterranean by German dive-bombers. The Red Cross markings on the fore and aft decks were no protection. Unarmed and helpless, the Aba was mercilessly bombed.

THE NAZI BRUTES. THEY MUST HAVE SEEN OUR RED CROSS MARKINGS YET STILL THEY BOMB US. SEND OUT AN SOS.

RADIO ROOM

IT'S THE HOSPITAL SHIP, ABA, SIR. SHE'S BEING ATTACKED BY DIVE BOMBERS!

CONTINUED ON BACK PAGE

The WIZARD

No. 1843—JUNE 10th, 1961.   PRICE 4d.

THE IDENTICAL ENEMIES!

ONE of them is a hardened Nazi tyrant, a cruel killer. The other is a man whose one aim is to seek vengeance on Nazi tyrants. Which one is which? The answer is in the super, last-war story of mystery and suspense—

RED VENGEANCE

GOOD !
good to eat...good for you

Good for a Merry Christmas too. "Good for you!" the family will shout when you bring out the Cadbury's Chocolate Biscuits. Make sure everyone enjoys Christmas with Cadbury's.

Cadbury's Chocolate Biscuits

COVERED WITH
CADBURY'S
'DAIRY MILK'
CHOCOLATE

FIVE FAVOURITES IN ONE PACKET **2/-** ■ ¼ lb.

RICE (Oryza Sativa)
One of the world's
most nourishing grains.

Civilized way to get the vigorous virtues of rice in the raw

Native rice is famous for its thiamine, niacin and iron.

Often lost in polished rice, these vital nutritional values are fully restored in Kellogg's Rice Krispies.

So crisp they go "Snap! Crackle! Pop!" when you pour on milk or cream. In cereal talk this means

"The best to you each morning."

Kellogg's

RICE KRISPIES

Now! Illuminated bus side signs made from 'Perspex'

Bus-side signs made from 'Perspex' acrylic sheet are now used on a number of buses belonging to the North Western Road Car Company Ltd., Stockport, a member of the B.E.T. Federation Ltd.

These bus-side signs are doing a hard selling job from early morning to midnight for advertisers in the Stockport area. Bright, colourful, backed by fluorescent lighting, the signs are really easy to read on the darkest night.

Each sign is 17 ft. 11½ ins. long and 21½ ins. deep and consists of three panels of $\frac{3}{16}$" clear 'Perspex' cut from 3 six-foot long sheets. The sheets are jointed by means of a cover strap system – a clear 'Perspex' strap is cemented to the panel nearest the front of the bus and the next panel is fitted underneath. The panels can easily be moved, but each joint is completely waterproof. The sign is mounted 1¾" clear of the inner skin to give room for ten two foot fluorescent tubes. These are run off the bus batteries, using a transistorised converter.

The advertising message can be screen printed on the inside of the sheets or, if the message has to be changed frequently, paper posters can be stuck onto the sheets.

'PERSPEX'

'Perspex' is the registered trade mark for the acrylic sheet manufactured by I.C.I.

ICI

IMPERIAL CHEMICAL INDUSTRIES LIMITED · LONDON · S.W.1

PB74

Punch, November 15 1961

ENTER··· THE NEW SHAPE OF

FANFARE! Roll away the work-a-day! Enter the *swish* new Anglia Estate. Is it exciting? You never saw an estate car so excitingly good-looking. Or sat in one so excitingly comfortable. Or drove one so excitingly energetic. That's because Ford said: Give the new estate car all the excitement of the de luxe Anglia Saloon ... *but in an entirely new estate-car shape.* So you get saloon-bred elegance, with luxury comfort for four adults. You get the rally-proved, highly-praised Anglia engine. That joy of a gear stick. And terrific cycloramic vision (thanks to vast all-round windows and *low* loading floor).

What else? Traditional Ford operating economy. 70-plus top speed. Separate front seats. Padded arm rests. And those wonderful Ford specials—easy hp, low insurance rates, fixed-cost country-wide service. See your Ford dealer *today.*

excitement!

THE NEW ANGLIA ESTATE CAR

De luxe model illustrated

Integral construction of bod
and chassis gives grea
strength and durabilit
throughout. Safety glass al
round. Soft padded sunvisor
Back seat folds down in
twink when you want t
give any amount of low an
therefore safe storage spac
The floor is neatly linoleum
covered and completely fla

Ex-works from

£679.7.3

(£465 + £214.7.3 pt.)
Over-riders optional extra.

WORLD'S MOST <u>EXCITING</u> ESTATE CAR FROM **FORD** OF BRITAIN

COST OF LIVING 1961

A conversion of pre-decimal to decimal money

The Pound, 1971 became the year of decimalization when the pound became 100 new pennies. Prior to that the pound was equivalent to 20 shillings. Money prior to 1971 was written £/s/d. (d being for pence). Below is a chart explaining the monetary value of each coin before and after 1971.

Symbol	Before 1971	After 1971
£	Pound (240 pennies)	Pound (100 new pennies)
s	Shilling (12 pennies)	5 pence
d	Penny	¼ of a penny
¼d	Farthing	1 penny
½d	Halfpenny	½ pence
3d	Threepence	About 1/80 of a pound
4d	Groat (four pennies)	
6d	Sixpence (Tanner)	2½ new pence
2s	Florin (2 shillings)	10 pence
2s/6d	Half a crown (2 shillings and 6 pence)	12½ pence
5s	Crown	25 pence
10s	10 shilling note (10 bob)	50 pence
10s/6d	½ Guinea	52½ pence
21s	1 Guinea	105 pence

Prices are in equivalent to new pence today and on average throughout the UK.

Item	1961	Price equivalent today
Wages, average yearly	£562.00	£11,692.00
Average house price	£2,403.00	£49,982.00
Price of an average car	£805.00	£16,744.00
Litre of petrol	£0.05p	£1.12p
Flour 1.5kg	£0.10p	£2.00p
Bread (loaf)	£0.05p	£1.10p
Sugar 1kg	£0.07p	£1.50p
Milk 1 pint	£0.13p	£2.75p
Butter 250g	£0.08p	£1.62p
Cheese 400g	£0.12p	£2.59p
Potatoes 2.5kg	£0.08p	£1.66p
Bacon 400g	£0.26p	£5.49p
Beer (Pint)	£0.08p	£1.64p

So what was £100 a week worth in 1961?

an age when footballers are rejecting £100,000-per-week contracts, the £100 weekly sum offered to Johnny ynes by Fulham in 1961 seems a rather paltry affair. But at a time when the average annual salary was just der £1,000, this income would have allowed you to live a life of relative luxury.

use prices in Harold Macmillan's England averaged £2,700 with a litre of four-star petrol costing a very sonable 5p. A carton of milk could be purchased for 4p while a pint of bitter from the Craven Cottage bar uld set you back a mere 8p.

th the Beatles yet to make their imprint outside the Cavern Club, the singles charts were dominated by the s of Del Shannon and the Everly Brothers while Elvis Presley had his ninth UK No 1 with His Latest Flame.

most successful film of 1961 was West Side Story, the New York-set Romeo and Juliet musical update bbing 10 Oscars.

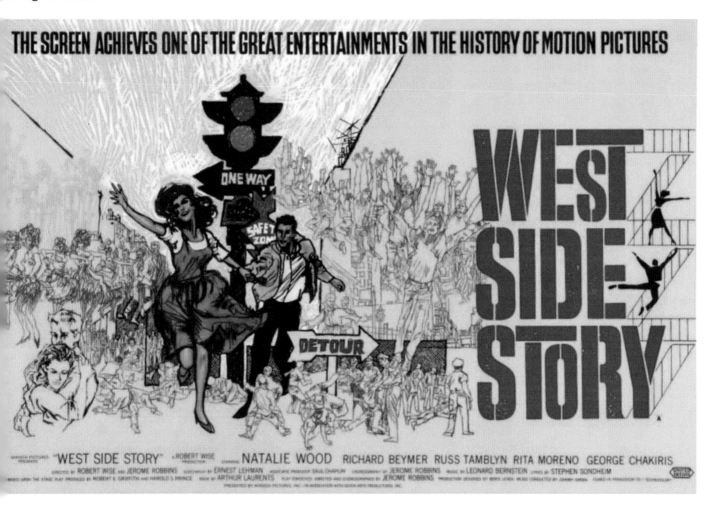

961 the life expectancy in United Kingdom decreased to 70.88 years.

year, the life expectancy for women was 73.9 years and for men 68 years.

ed Kingdom's position worsened dropping from the 9th in 1960 to 13th in 1961.

BRITISH BIRTHS

Fiona Phillips was born on the 1st January 1961and grew up in Canterbury, Kent She is an English journalist, broadcaster and television presenter. Fiona Phillips started her career in independent radio working as a reporter for local stations County Sound in Surrey, Hereward Radio and Radio Mercury in Sussex. Moving from radio to television several years later, she joined BBC South East's Weeken programme as co-presenter, before becoming a reporter with CNN News, later moving on to become the station's entertainment editor, producing, reporting a presenting CNN News' entertainment output. Fiona has presented other programmes, including the celebrity lifestyle show OK!TV, Baby House and Roo Rent, Carlton's entertainment guide Good Stuff, LWT's Friday evening entertainment show Start the Weekend, ITV's Sunday Night and the Rich and Famous series. She was a regular panellist on Loose Women in 2002, and was a guest anchor in 2004 and 2005. She returned to Loose Women as a guest ancho March 2009 and again in March 2010.

Neil Dudgeon was born on the 2nd January 1961and was born in Doncaster, West Riding of Yorkshire, England. Neil who is an actor made his first screen appearance in 1987. The following year he appeared as a Second World War pilot in Piece of Cake, alongside Tim Woodward. As well as occasional appearances in series such as Casualty, London's Burning and Lovejoy, he appeared in 1994 as Detective Constable Costello, a one-episode subordinate to Detective Inspector William Edward "Jack" Frost (played by David Jason), in the TV series A Touch of Frost. In 2010 Neil appeared in an episode of the ITV crime drama Midsomer Murders, called "The Sword of Guillaume". He was introduced in the episode as the cousin of Detective Chief Inspector Tom Barnaby, played by John Nettles, who retired from the role. Neil, also cast as a senior detective, took over as the lead character in Midsomer Murders after the last episodes featuring John Nettles were screened in 2011. In 2012 Dudgeon starred as Norman Birkett on BBC Radio 4's Afternoon Play series in four plays written by Caroline and David Stafford based on Birkett's cases.

Ian Cameron Mercer was born the 10th July 1961. Ian grew up in Oldham, Lancashire, England and wanted to become an actor. Ian went on to work in s stage productions as Bent, Spend Spend Spend, Saturday Night, Sunday Morr Billy Liar, Stop The Children's Laughter, Welcome Home, Romeo and Juliet, Th Fancy Man, The York Realist, Beauty and the Beast and Revengers Tragedy. H television and film acting credits include leading roles in Starting Out, (1982), series made by ATV for schools and written by Grazyna Monvid, Coronation Street (as Gary Mallett and in 1987, Pete Jackson), Shackleton (with Kenneth Branagh), Heartbeat, The Monocled Mutineer, A Touch of Frost, Cracker, Common As Muck, Peak Practice and New Tricks. In 2009 he appeared in an episode of Doctors and two episodes of Waking the Dead. He appeared as Blackbeard's chief zombie henchman in Pirates of the Caribbean: On Stranger Tides. During August and September 2015 he returned to Doctors playing the recurring role of Andy Weston in an ongoing sub-plot.

Graham McPherson was born on the 13th January 1961 and grew up in Hastings, Sussex, England. He is known by the stage name Suggs and is an English singer-songwriter, musician, radio personality and actor. Suggs got his nickname from randomly sticking a pin in an encyclopaedia of jazz musicians hitting Peter Suggs. In 1976 Mike Barson, Chris Foreman and Lee Thompson formed the North London Invaders, which later became the band Madness. In a music career spanning 40 years, Suggs came to prominence in the late 1970s as the lead singer of the ska band Madness, which released fifteen singles that entered the Top 10 charts in the United Kingdom during the 1970s, 1980s and the 1990s, including "My Girl", "Baggy Trousers", "Embarrassment", "It Must Be Love", "House of Fun", "Driving in My Car", "Our House", "Wings of a Dove" and "Lovestruck". Suggs began his solo career in 1995, while still a member of Madness. Since then, he has released two studio albums and two compilation albums. His solo hits include "I'm Only Sleeping", "Camden Town", "Cecilia" and "Blue Day".

er Andrew Beardsley MBE was born on the 18th January 1961 and grew up in ham, Northumberland, England. Peter Beardsley signed for Newcastle for a of £150,000, although when they had let him go earlier they could have ed him for nothing. Peter was an instant hit with the Newcastle supporters, ring and setting up spectacular goals. He went on to celebrate promotion h his teammates, who were captained by Kevin Keegan in his final season as a er. He scored 20 league goals that season and formed an exciting strike tnership with former England striker Kevin Keegan who had also won major ours with Liverpool. . At club level, he played for Newcastle United, Liverpool Everton, having also had spells with Carlisle United, Manchester United, couver Whitecaps, Bolton Wanderers, Manchester City, Fulham, Hartlepool ted and the Melbourne Knights. He was briefly appointed as the caretaker ager of Newcastle United in 2010. After reaching the First Division with castle, Beardsley became a regular in the England side in the second half of 1980s, and teamed up with striker Gary Lineker.

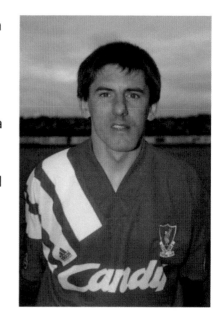

Andrew Arthur Taylor was born on the 16th February 1961 and grew up in Cullercoats, Northumberland, England. He began playing guitar at the age of eleven, and was soon playing with local bands, even producing one at the age of sixteen. After six years of being a member of Duran Duran, Taylor had realised both he and the band were in free fall. He and the other band members rarely spoke to one another and the band were now living in three different continents. Andy Taylor himself was now based in Los Angeles where he met with ex-Sex Pistols guitarist Steve Jones and they began collaborating for Taylor's forthcoming solo album. Throughout 1987 and 1988, Taylor co-wrote and co-produced Rod Stewart's multi-Platinum album Out of Order along with Chic members Bernard Edwards and Tony Thompson. Andy Taylor then moved on to producing full-time, working with several successful UK bands throughout the 1990s. In 2001, Taylor reunited with the other original members of Duran Duran to record their first new music together since 1985. The band secured a new recording contract with Sony Records.

Justinus Soni "Justin" Fashanu was born on the 19th February 1961 and sadly passed away on the 2nd May 1998. Justin Fashanu began his career as an apprentice with Norwich City, turning professional towards the end of December 1978. He made his league debut on 13th January 1979, against We Bromwich Albion, and settled into the Norwich side scoring regularly and occasionally spectacularly. In 1980, he won the BBC Goal of the Season award for a spectacular goal against Liverpool. He managed a total of 103 senior appearances for Norwich, scoring 40 goals. In October 1990, he publicly came out as gay in an interview with the tabloid press, becoming the only prominent player in English football so far to do so. On the morning of 3 May, he was for hanged in a deserted lock-up garage he had broken into, in Fairchild Place, Shoreditch, London. In his suicide note, he denied the charges, stating that the sex was consensual, and that he had fled to England because he felt he could not get a fair trial because of his homosexuality.

Fatima Whitbread MBE, born Fatima Vedad on the 3rd March 1961. Fatima was born in Stoke Newington, London. At the age of 14, she was adopted by the family of Margaret Whitbread, her javelin coach. Whitbread broke the javelin world record with a throw of 77.44m in the qualifying round of the 1986 European Championships in Athletics (where she also won the final) and became World Champion in 1987. She became well known in the UK for her celebratory wiggle after defeating arch-rival Petra Felke in these events. Her performances in 1987 led to her being voted winner of the BBC Sports Personality of the Year award. Fatima had won the silver medal at the inaugural World Championships in 1983. She was also known for her rivalry with fellow British javelin thrower Tessa Sanderson, who won the gold medal at the 1984 Summer Olympics in Los Angeles with Whitbread finishing in bronze medal position. Starting on 13 November 2011, Whitbread took part in the ITV show I'm a Celebrity...Get Me Out of Here! Fatima Whitbread and fellow camp mate Antony Cotton left after 21 days.

William Jefferson Hague, Baron Hague of Richmond, PC, FRSL was bo on the 26th March 1961 and grew up in Rotherham, Yorkshire, England first made the national news at the age of 16 by addressing the Conservatives at their 1977 Annual National Conference. Hague read Philosophy, Politics and Economics at Magdalen College, Oxford, graduating with first-class honours. He was President of the Oxford University Conservative Association (OUCA), but was "convicted of electoral malpractice" in the election process. Following the 1997 gen election defeat, Hague was elected Leader of the Conservative Party i succession to John Major, defeating more experienced figures such as Kenneth Clarke and Michael Howard. At the age of 36, Hague was tas with rebuilding the Conservative Party (fresh from their worst general election result of the 20th century) by attempting to build a more mo image. £250,000 was spent on the "Listening to Britain" campaign to t put the Conservatives back in touch with the public after losing powe

Ellery Cuthwyn Hanley MBE was born on the 27th March 1961 and from Leeds, West Riding of Yorkshire, England. Over a nineteen-year professional career (1978-1997), he played for Bradford Northern, Wigan, Balmain, Western Suburbs and Leeds. He won 36 caps for Great Britain, captaining the team from 1988 to 1992, and 2 for England. Nicknamed 'Mr Magic' and 'The Black Pearl', he played most often as a stand-off or loose forward after starting out as a centre or wing. Hanley won the Man of Steel Award a record three times, the Lance Todd Trophy once and the Golden Boot in 1988. He was awarded the MBE in January 1990 for services to the game. In 2005 he was inducted into the Rugby Football League Hall of Fame. After his playing career, he had spells as head coach of Great Britain, St Helens and Doncaster. In 2009 Hanley was one of thirteen celebrities taking part in the new series of Dancing on Ice, partnered with Frankie Poultney. He was the sixth person to be eliminated from the show, after falling on the ice during the final dance-off.

an Magdalane Boyle was on the born 1st April 1961 and grew up in ckburn, West Lothian, Scotland. She is a Scottish singer, who rose to fame er appearing as a contestant on the third series of Britain's Got Talent, ging "I Dreamed a Dream" from Les Misérables. Susan's first album, I amed a Dream, was released on 23 November 2009. The album includes ers of "Wild Horses" and "You'll See" as well as "I Dreamed a Dream", and y Me a River". In Britain, Boyle's debut album was recognised as the fastest ing UK debut album of all time selling 411,820 copies, beating the previous est selling debut of all time, Spirit by Leona Lewis. I Dreamed a Dream also sold the rest of the top 5 albums combined in its first week. On the 9th July 0, Boyle announced that her second album would be a Christmas album itled The Gift. As part of the lead-up to the album, she held a competition ed Susan's Search, the winner of which sang a duet with her on her new CD. album was released on the 8th November 2010. Susan has now released 6 ums in total.

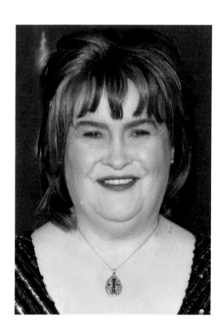

Roderick Keith Ogilvy "Rory" Bremner, was born on the 6th April 1961 and from Edinburgh, Scotland. Rory is a Scottish impressionist and comedian, noted for his work in political satire and impressions of British public figures. He is also known for his work on Mock the Week as a panellist (for Series 1 and 2), award-winning show Rory Bremner...Who Else? and sketch comedy series Bremner, Bird and Fortune. Rory Bremner has translated three operas into English: Der Silbersee by Kurt Weill, Carmen by Georges Bizet, and Orpheus in the Underworld by Jacques Offenbach. In April 2007, he took part in The Big Brecht Fest at the Young Vic Theatre in London celebrating the work of German dramatist Bertolt Brecht. In 2015, he returned to TV comedy with two political satire programmes on BBC Two: "Rory Bremner's Coalition Report", a satirical summary of the previous five years in British Politics, and the "Election Report", a satire of the 2015 General Election. From 2016, Bremner has been a team captain on the ITV comedy game show The Imitation Game, a panel show hosted by Alexander Armstrong based around impressions.

Robert Carlyle OBE was born on the 14th April 1961 and grew up in Maryhill, Glasgow, Scotland. In 1994, he played the gay lover of Father Greg in the film Priest. Carlyle's first high-profile role came as murderer Albert "Albie" Kinsella an October 1994 episode of Cracker opposite Robbie Coltrane and Christopher Eccleston. This highly acclaimed role showcased Carlyle's "pure intensity". Sho after his appearance in Cracker, he landed the role of Highland policeman Ham Macbeth in the BBC comedy-drama Hamish Macbeth. The series ran for three seasons from 1995 to 1997. In 1996 and 1997, he appeared in the two highest profile roles of his career to date: as the psychopathic Francis Begbie in Trainspotting and Gaz, the leader of a group of amateur male strippers, in The Monty. The latter earned Robert Carlyle a BAFTA Award for Best Actor in a Leading Role. He also starred with Ray Winstone in the 1997 film Face. From 2 to 2018, Carlyle portrayed Mr. Gold (Rumpelstiltskin) in the fantasy-drama television series Once Upon A Time. The character is a wizard, deal-maker, and master manipulator.

Nicholas Simon Lyndhurst was born on the 20th April 1961 and grew up in Emsworth, Hampshire, England. Nicholas Lyndhurst appeared in various television adverts and children's films in the late 1970s, before landing a main character role in The Prince and the Pauper in 1976. He first gained national recognition at the age of seventeen in the sitcom Butterflies written by Carla Lane, in which he played Adam Parkinson. He then played Raymond Fletcher, the teenage son of Norman Stanley Fletcher played by Ronnie Barker in Going Straight, followed by Dobson in the BBC TV series To Serve Them All My Days. He achieved national stardom in the series Only Fools and Horses in which he played Rodney Trotter, the younger brother of the main character Derek "Del Boy" Trotter. Only Fools and Horses began in 1981 and rapidly grew in popularity until it reached its peak in 1996 with its Christmas Day show in the UK. From 1993 to 1999, he played the complex lead character of Gary Sparrow in the fantasy sitcom Goodnight Sweetheart. In 2013 he joined the cast as a regular of Series 10 of New Tricks.

Philip Vickery was born on the 2nd May 1961 and from Folkestone, Kent, England. He is an English celebrity chef. He is best known for working on ITV's This Morning, where he has been the Chef since 2006. Phil Vickery followed Gary Rhodes as head chef of the Castle Hotel, Taunton, Somers which at the time held a Michelin Star. It lost its Michelin status under Vickery, but retained its 4 AA rosettes, while he gained the AA Chef of th Year. Vickery regained the Michelin star, re-awarded for four consecutiv years from 1994 to 1997. Vickery has written twelve books. The first, "Ju Food", was published by Headline in 1999. He appeared in BBC's Ready Steady Cook over 200 times between 1996 and 2010 until the show's retirement. In September 2008, Vickery began advertising food product and promoting special offers for supermarket chain Aldi, after signing a year deal with the chain. He is also the current spokesperson for Unileve Stork brand margarine. He is married to Fern Britton, has one daughter Winifred and is stepfather to Fern's three children from her first marriag

Timothy Simon Roth was born on the 14th May 1961 and grew up in Dulwich, London, England. Tom is an English actor and director. Tom Roth made his acting début at the age of 21, playing a white supremacist skinhead named Trevor in a 1982 TV film titled Made in Britain. Tom Roth and other young British actors of the late 1980s, such as Gary Oldman, Colin Firth, Daniel Day-Lewis, Bruce Payne, and Paul McGann, were dubbed the Brit Pack. Roth was cast as "Mr. Orange" in Quentin Tarantino's 1992 film Reservoir Dogs. In 1994, Tarantino cast him as a robber in Pulp Fiction. In 2001, he portrayed General Thade in Tim Burton's Planet of the Apes. Roth was the original choice for the role of Severus Snape in the Harry Potter film series, but he turned it down for Planet of the Apes. He was considered for the part of Hannibal Lecter in the 2001 film Hannibal before Anthony Hopkins returned to reclaim the role. He appeared in Francis Ford Coppola's Youth Without Youth and Michael Haneke's Funny Games, and then starred as Emil Blonsky / Abomination, a Russian-born officer in the United Kingdom's Royal Marines Commandos, in The Incredible Hulk.

e **Darren Allen** was born on the 20th May 1961and grew up in Stepney,
don, England. He started his career at Queens Park Rangers in the late
'0s, and scored 32 league goals in 49 appearances, before moving to
enal. Clive Allen signed for Arsenal in the summer of 1980 for a fee of
25m, but he did not play a single competitive. He shortly moved on to
stal Palace in a swap deal with Kenny Sansom. He moved to Tottenham for
'00,000 fee. Allen scored twice on his debut on 25 August 1984, a 4-1
iy win at Everton, and scored 10 goals from 18 appearances in his first
son, in which Spurs finished third behind Liverpool and Everton. In 1986–
ie scored 33 League goals, and 49 goals in all competitions. He also picked
:he titles of PFA Player of the Year and Football Writers' Association
tballer of the Year. He ended his career with three league games for
lisle United in 1995–96. In the summer of 1984, Allen was given his first
land cap against Brazil. In total he made five appearances for England.

Boy George, born George Alan O'Dowd on the 14th June 1961. George grew up in Barnehurst, Kent, England. He is an English singer, songwriter, DJ and fashion designer. He is the lead singer of the pop band Culture Club. At the height of the band's fame, during the 1980s, they recorded global hit songs such as "Karma Chameleon", "Do You Really Want to Hurt Me" and "Time (Clock of the Heart)". George is known for his soulful voice and his androgynous appearance. He was part of the English New Romantic movement which emerged in the late 1970s to the early 1980s. His music is often classified as blue-eyed soul, which is influenced by rhythm and blues and reggae. He was lead singer of Jesus Loves You during the period 1989–1992. His 1990s and 2000s-era solo music has glam influences, such as David Bowie and Iggy Pop. More recently, he has released fewer music recordings, splitting his time between song writing, DJing, writing books, designing clothes and photography. In 2015, Boy George received an Ivor Novello Award from the British Academy of Songwriters, Composers and Authors for Outstanding Services to British Music.

Geneviève Alison Jane Moyet was born on the 18th June 1961 and is an English singer, songwriter and performer noted for her powerful bluesy contralto voice. She was born in Billericay, Essex, England, United Kingdor At the age of 21, Moyet's mainstream pop career began in 1982 with the formation of the synthpop duo Yazoo with former Depeche Mode membe Vince Clarke. Yazoo had several hits, including "Only You", "Don't Go", "Situation" and "Nobody's Diary", and recorded two albums, Upstairs at E and You and Me Both. Moyet signed to CBS, and began her solo career. In 1984, Moyet released her debut solo album Alf. In August 2002, Moyet w. released from her Sony contract. Moyet signed to Sanctuary Records and released her first studio album in eight years. Moyet made her stage debu the London West End production of the musical Chicago in 2001. She play the part of Matron 'Mama' Morton, and although it had initially been intended to be a short run, it eventually ran for six months.

Ricky Dene Gervais was born on the 25th June 1961 and grew up in Reading, Berkshire, England. Ricky is an English stand-up comedian, actor, writer, film producer, director, and musician. He is perhaps best known for co-creating, writing, and acting in the British television series The Office. He has won seven BAFTA Awards, five British Comedy Awards, two Emmy Awards, three Golden Globe Awards, and the Rose d'Or twice (2006 and 2019), as well as a Screen Actors Guild Award nomination. In 2007, he was placed at No. 11 on Channel 4's 100 Greatest Stand-Ups and at No. 3 on the updated 2010 list. In 2010, he was named on the Time 100 list of the world's most influential people. Extras had its debut on the BBC on the 21st July 2005; directed by Ricky Gervais and Stephen Merchant, the sitcom ran for twelve episodes and starred Gervais as Andy Millman, a background artist. An Idiot Abroad is a travel documentary produced by Gervais and Merchant where a reluctant Karl Pilkington travels around the world, with his reactions to people and places recorded. Occasionally, Gervais and Merchant call to surprise him with a new place to visit or task to do.

Suzanne Jane Dando, BEM was born on the 3rd July 1961 and from Balha London and is a former British Olympic gymnast, who competed at the 1 World Gymnastics Championship. Her gymnastics talent was first recogn at age eleven by her school physical education teacher Anne Billingham. quickly passed all the BAGA awards and climbed onto the uneven bars fc the first time when she was 12. In 1980, Dando won the 'Champion of Champions' title at the Royal Albert Hall. In May she became the Overall British National Champion. She led her teammates, Susan Cheesborougl and Denise Jones, to the 1980 Olympics in Moscow. Dando improved dramatically on her standing (48th) following prelims, finishing 27th in tl AA competition. Following her retirement, Dando coached the under-fiv gymnastics at the Lewisham Leisure Centre in South London. She wrote book, "Fun Ways to Looking Good", and produced and presented her ov fitness video, "Flexercise". In the early 1980s, she made several appeara for the Conservative Party, citing Margaret Thatcher as her inspiration.

Brian Paul Conley was born on the 7th August 1961 and is an English comedian, television presenter, singer and actor. In 1992, LWT offered him another opportunity to star in his own comedy programme, with The Brian Conley Show. At the suggestion of producer and director Nigel Lythgoe, this new show had a variety format rather than being purely sketches. This different format proved popular, and the show became Britain's most-watched light entertainment programme. Conley's next success was a sitcom entitled Time After Time, in which he played the lead role. The show was named 'Best ITV Sitcom' at the 1994 British Comedy Awards. In 2006, Conley returned to television, hosting a daytime variety show called Let Me Entertain You, a Lion TV production for BBC Two where 13-year-old operatic baritone Matthew Crane was the first series champion. On the 1st December of the same year, he appeared as a guest presenter on The New Paul O'Grady Show on Channel 4, where Larry the Loafer made an appearance in the beginning, and Brian referred himself to "Dangerous Brian".

on **Weston CBE** was born on the 8th August 1961 and born in Caerphilly, morgan, Wales. He joined the Welsh Guards in 1978 at the age of 16 at the stence of his mother, after he "got into bother". He served in Berlin, thern Ireland and Kenya before being deployed to the Falkland Islands. On 8th June 1982, he was boarded with other members of his regiment on RFA Galahad in Port Pleasant near Fitzroy, just off the Falkland Islands. It was nbed and set on fire by the Argentine Skyhawk fighters during the Bluff Cove Attacks. His ship was carrying ammunition as well as phosphorus bombs and usands of gallons of diesel and petrol. Out of his platoon of 30 men, 22 were ed. The Welsh Guards lost a total of 48 men killed and 97 wounded aboard Sir Galahad. Simon Weston endured years of reconstructive surgery, uding over 96 major operations or surgical procedures. In 1986 Simon ston undertook his first goodwill tour, to Australia, at the request of the rds Association of Australasia. The resulting donations to children's burns s made him begin to feel useful again.

Martin John Kemp was born on the 10th October 1961 and from Islington, England. Kemp's life changed when Steve Dagger, the manager of his brother Gary's band the Gentry, suggested he should replace the band's bass player. Kemp learned to play bass in three months and performed for the first time with the Gentry at a college party. Eventually the band was renamed "Spandau Ballet" and Kemp left his printing job to concentrate on the band full-time. Spandau Ballet went on to have a great deal of success in the New Romantic Era, with four of their albums reaching the UK album chart top ten. Martin Kemp and his brother Gary returned to acting in 1990, both of them appearing in the British film The Krays, in which they played the notorious gangster twins Ronald and Reginald Kray. He resumed his acting career in 1998 when he made a guest appearance in the ITV police drama series The Bill. He went on to become popular for his role as villain Steve Owen in the BBC's top soap opera, EastEnders from December 1998. In December 2017 he appeared as Captain Hook in Peter Pan.

Diana Frances Spencer, Princess of Wales was born on the 1st July 1961 and tragically passed away on the 31st August 1997. She was the first wife of Charles, Prince of Wales, and the mother of Prince William and Prince Harry. Diana's activism and glamour made her an international icon and earned her an enduring popularity as well as an unprecedented public scrutiny, exacerbated by her tumultuous private life.

Diana came to prominence in 1981 upon her engagement to Prince Charles, the eldest son of Queen Elizabeth after a brief courtship. Their wedding took place at St Paul's Cathedral in 1981 and made her Princess of Wales role in which she was enthusiastically received by the public. The couple had two sons, the princes William and Harry, who were then second and third in the line of succession to the British throne. Diana's marriage to Charles however, suffered due to their incompatibility and extramarital affairs. The couple separated in 1992, soon after the breakdown of their relationship became public knowledge. The details of their marital difficulties became increasingly publicised, and the marriage ended in divorce in 1996.

As Princess of Wales, Diana undertook royal duties on behalf of the Queen and represented her at functions across the Commonwealth realms. She was celebrated in the media for her unconventional approach to charity work. Her patronages initially centered on children and youth but she later became known for her involvement with AIDS patients and campaign for the removal of landmines. She also raised awareness and advocated ways help people affected with cancer and mental illness. As princess, Diana was initially noted for her shyness, but charisma and friendliness endeared her to the public and helped her reputation survive the acrimonious collapse of her marriage. Considered to be very photogenic, she was a leader of fashion in the 1980s and 1990s. Media attention and public mourning were extensive after her death in a car crash in a Paris tunnel in 1997 and subsequent televised funeral. Her legacy has had a deep impact on the royal family and British society.

On the 31st August 1997, Diana died in a car crash in the Pont de l'Alma tunnel in Paris while the driver was fleeing the paparazzi. The crash also resulted in the deaths of her companion Dodi Fayed and the driver, Henri Paul, who was the acting security manager of the Hôtel Ritz Paris. Diana's bodyguard, Trevor Rees-Jones, survived the crash. The televised funeral, on 6 September, was watched by a British television audience that peaked at 32.10 million, which was one of the United Kingdom's highest viewing figures ever. Millions more watched the event around the world.

BRITISH DEATHS

Morris Stanley "Stan" Nichols was born on the 6th October 1900 and passed away on the 26th January 1961. Stanley was born in Stondon Massey, Essex, England and was primarily a football goalkeeper who played for some time with Queen's Park Rangers. Stan Nichols' prowess at cricket during the summer brought him to the attention of the Essex committee during the early 1920s, who recommended him as a left-handed batsman. 1926 was Nichols' breakthrough year, for he took 114 wickets in first-class cricket. In 1927 Nichols took 124 wickets for 23 runs each, with several strong performances: including nine for 59 against Hampshire at Chelmsford; eight for 46 against Derbyshire at Southend; and nine for 32 against Somerset at Colchester. 1936 saw Nichols make his only double century, against Hampshire, and take nine for 32 against Nottinghamshire at Trent Bridge, whilst 1937 and 1938 were seasons of consistent achievement culminating in an all-round performance of 159 and fifteen for 163 against Gloucestershire in the latter season.

orge Formby, OBE born George Hoy Booth on the 26th May 1904 and
ly died on the 6th March 1961. Born in Wigan, Lancashire, he was the son
George Formby Sr, from whom he later took his stage name. After an
ly career as a stable boy and jockey, George Formby took to the music
 stage after the early death of his father in 1921. In 1923 he made two
eer-changing decisions – he purchased a ukulele, and married Beryl
nam, a fellow performer who became his manager and transformed his
 During the Second World War Formby worked extensively for the
ertainments National Service Association (ENSA), and entertained
ians and troops, and by 1946 it was estimated that he had performed in
 nt of three million service personnel. His last television appearance was
ecember 1960, two weeks before the death of Beryl. He surprised
ple by announcing his engagement to a school teacher seven weeks
 r Beryl's funeral, but died in Preston three weeks later, at the age of 56;
vas buried in Warrington, alongside his father.

Belinda Lee born on the 15th June 1935 and died on the 12th March 1961 and was an English actress. Born in Budleigh Salterton, Devon, Belinda Lee was signed to a film contract in 1954 by the Rank Studios after being seen performing as a student of the Royal Academy of Dramatic Art. She made her film debut opposite comic Frankie Howerd (in his film debut) in The Runaway Bus (1954). Rank finally gave Lee a good chance, casting her as a nurse in a medical drama The Feminine Touch (1956). She followed this with a crime drama The Secret Place (1957) and Miracle in Soho (1957). She was an aristocrat helping Louis Jourdan in Dangerous Exile (1957), during the filming of which she was injured when her hair caught fire. She returned to Rank Studios to make Nor the Moon by Night (1957) which was shot on location in South Africa. During filming, Lee left to go to Italy to visit her married lover. In 1961, Belinda Lee died in a car accident near San Bernardino, California, on her way to Los Angeles from Las Vegas, where she had been acting in a film. Her ashes are interred in the Non-Catholic Cemetery in Rome, Italy.

Richard H. Dale was born on the 25th April 1927 and died on the 30th April 1961 Hewas known as Dickie Dale and was a Grand Prix motorcycle road rac

He was born in Wyberton near Boston, Lincolnshire, England. In 1945 he wa drafted into the RAF and served as a flight mechanic, and bought his first motorcycle, a 1939 AJS Silver Streak, while stationed at RAF Cranwell.

He competed in the inaugural 1949 Grand Prix motorcycle racing season. D was a victor in the 1951 North West 200. His best seasons were 1955 and 1 when he finished in second place in the 350cc world championship, both ti behind his Moto Guzzi teammate Bill Lomas.

Dale also competed in the 500cc class aboard Moto Guzzi's famous V8 Gra Prix bike. He died on the way to hospital in an unpressurized helicopter, aft crashing during the 1961 Eifelrennen race at Nürburgring, Germany.

Herbert John "Bert" Pitman MBE. He was born on the 20th November 1877 and passed away on the 7th December 1961. Herbert Pitman was born in the Somerset village of Sutton Montis in England. Herbert Pitman first went to sea in 1895 at the age of 18 after joining the Merchant Navy. He received the shore part of his nautical training in the Navigation Department of the Merchant Ventures' Technical College, under Mr. E. F. White, and qualified as a Master Mariner in August 1906. Like the other junior officers Pitman received a telegram early in 1912 directing him to report to White Star's Liverpool office at nine in the morning on the 26th March of that year. At the time of the Titanic's collision with the iceberg, Pitman was off-duty, half-asleep in his bunk in the Officers' Quarters. Pitman continued to serve with the White Star Line following the Titanic disaster. He served on the liners RMS Oceanic and Titanic's older sister Olympic. Pitman died of a subarachnoid haemorrhage on the 7th December 1961 at the age of 84 years. His body was buried in the graveyard of Pitcombe Parish Church, Somerset.

Harriet Shaw Weaver was born on the 1st September 1876 and die the 14th October 1961 and was a political activist and a magazine editor. Harriet Shaw Weaver was born in Frodsham, Cheshire, the s of eight children of Frederic Poynton Weaver. In 1911 she began subscribing to The Freewoman: A Weekly Feminist Review, a radica periodical. In 1913 it was renamed The New Freewoman. Later tha year at the suggestion of the magazine's literary editor, Ezra Pound name was changed again to The Egoist.

In 1931 Weaver joined the Labour Party but then, having been influenced by reading Marx's Das Kapital she joined the Communis Party in 1938. She was active in this organisation, taking part in demonstrations and selling copies of the Daily Worker. She also continued her allegiance to the memory of Joyce, acting as his liter executor and helping to compile The Letters of James Joyce. She di at her home near Saffron Walden in 1961, aged 85.

SPORTING EVENTS 1961

1961 County Cricket Season

npshire County Cricket Club wins the County Championship for the
t time. One of eighteen first-class county clubs within the domestic
ket structure of England and Wales. It represents the historic county
Hampshire. Hampshire teams formed by earlier organisations,
ncipally the Hambledon Club, always had first-class status and the
e applied to the county club when it was founded in 1863. Because of
r performances for several seasons until 1885, Hampshire then lost its
us for nine seasons until it was invited into the County Championship
895, since when the team have played in every top-level domestic
ket competition in England. Hampshire originally played at the
elope Ground, Southampton until 1885 when they relocated to the
nty Ground, Southampton until 2000, before moving to the purpose-
t Rose Bowl in West End, which is in the Borough of Eastleigh. The
has twice won the County Championship, in the 1961 and 1973
ons.

Team	Pld	Won	Lost	Drawn	No Decision	1st Inns Loss	1st Inns Draw	Bonus	Points	Average
Hampshire	32	19	7	6	0	1	3	32	268	8.37
Yorkshire	32	17	5	10	0	1	5	34	250	7.81
Middlesex	28	15	6	6	1	3	1	26	214	7.64
Worcestershire	32	16	9	7	0	2	3	24	226	7.06
Gloucestershire	28	11	11	5	1	2	2	18	158	5.64
Essex	28	10	8	10	0	2	4	26	158	5.64
Derbyshire	28	10	9	9	0	3	3	22	154	5.50
Sussex	32	11	10	11	0	1	8	20	170	5.31
Leicestershire	28	9	13	5	1	2	4	26	146	5.21
Somerset	32	10	15	7	0	6	3	24	162	5.06
Kent	28	8	8	12	0	1	7	20	132	4.71
Warwickshire	32	9	10	13	0	1	7	26	150	4.68
Lancashire	32	9	7	15	1	1	7	18	142	4.43
Glamorgan	32	9	12	11	0	1	4	10	128	4.00
Surrey	28	4	13	11	0	6	8	24	100	3.57
Northamptonshire	28	5	13	10	0	1	5	10	82	2.92
Nottinghamshire	28	4	20	4	0	6	2	12	76	2.71

County Championship table

1960–61 in English football

The 1960–61 season was the 81st season of competitive football in England. This season was a particularly historic one for domestic football in England, as Tottenham Hotspur became the first club in the twentieth century to "do the Double" by winning both the League and the FA Cup competitions in the same season. Tottenham Hotspur sealed the Football League First Division title with a 2–1 home win over Sheffield Wednesday on the 17th April 1961. Preston North End, who had been the first team to achieve the League and FA Cup "double", was relegated in last place – and to date have not returned to the top flight of English football since. 1960–61 still remains the last time Tottenham Hotspur won the League Championship. Tottenham Hotspur beat Leicester City 2–0 to win the 1961 FA Cup Final at Wembley Stadium to become the first team in the 20th Century to win the double.

Pos	Team	Pld	W	D	L	GF	GA	GR	Pts	Qualification or relegation
1	Tottenham Hotspur	42	31	4	7	115	55	2.091	66	Qualified for the European Cup
2	Sheffield Wednesday	42	23	12	7	78	47	1.660	58	
3	Wolverhampton Wanderers	42	25	7	10	103	75	1.373	57	
4	Burnley	42	22	7	13	102	77	1.325	51	
5	Everton	42	22	6	14	87	69	1.261	50	
6	Leicester City	42	18	9	15	87	70	1.243	45	
7	Manchester United	42	18	9	15	88	76	1.158	45	
8	Blackburn Rovers	42	15	13	14	77	76	1.013	43	
9	Aston Villa	42	17	9	16	78	77	1.013	43	
10	West Bromwich Albion	42	18	5	19	67	71	0.944	41	
11	Arsenal	42	15	11	16	77	85	0.906	41	
12	Chelsea	42	15	7	20	98	100	0.980	37	
13	Manchester City	42	13	11	18	79	90	0.878	37	
14	Nottingham Forest	42	14	9	19	62	78	0.795	37	
15	Cardiff City	42	13	11	18	60	85	0.706	37	
16	West Ham United	42	13	10	19	77	88	0.875	36	
17	Fulham	42	14	8	20	72	95	0.758	36	
18	Bolton Wanderers	42	12	11	19	58	73	0.795	35	
19	Birmingham City	42	14	6	22	62	84	0.738	34	
20	Blackpool	42	12	9	21	68	73	0.932	33	
21	Newcastle United	42	11	10	21	86	109	0.789	32	Relegated to the Second Division
22	Preston North End	42	10	10	22	43	71	0.606	30	

1960–61 Scottish Division One & Two

The 1960–61 Scottish Division One was won by Rangers, who finished one point ahead of nearest rival Kilmarnock. Clyde and Ayr United finished 17th and 18th respectively and were relegated to the 1961-62 Second Division.

Pos	Team	Pld	W	D	L	GF	GA	GR	Pts
1	Rangers (C)	34	23	5	6	88	46	1.913	51
2	Kilmarnock	34	21	8	5	77	45	1.711	50
3	Third Lanark	34	20	2	12	100	80	1.250	42
4	Celtic	34	15	9	10	64	46	1.391	39
5	Motherwell	34	15	8	11	70	57	1.228	38
6	Aberdeen	34	14	8	12	72	72	1.000	36
7	Hearts	34	13	8	13	51	53	0.962	34
8	Hibernian	34	15	4	15	66	69	0.957	34
9	Dundee United	34	13	7	14	60	58	1.034	33
10	Dundee	34	13	6	15	61	53	1.151	32
11	Partick Thistle	34	13	6	15	59	69	0.855	32
12	Dunfermline Athletic	34	12	7	15	65	81	0.802	31
13	Airdrieonians	34	10	10	14	61	71	0.859	30
14	St Mirren	34	11	7	16	53	58	0.914	29
15	St Johnstone	34	10	9	15	47	63	0.746	29
16	Raith Rovers	34	10	7	17	46	67	0.687	27
17	Clyde (R)	34	6	11	17	55	77	0.714	23
18	Ayr United (R)	34	5	12	17	51	81	0.630	22

The 1960–61 Scottish Second Division was won by Stirling Albion who, along with second placed Falkirk, were promoted to the First Division. Morton finished bottom.

Pos	Team	Pld	W	D	L	GF	GA	GD	Pts
1	Stirling Albion	36	24	7	5	89	37	+52	55
2	Falkirk	36	24	6	6	100	40	+60	54
3	Stenhousemuir	36	24	2	10	99	69	+30	50
4	Stranraer	36	19	6	11	83	55	+28	44
5	Queen of the South	36	20	3	13	77	52	+25	43
6	Hamilton Academical	36	17	7	12	84	80	+4	41
7	Montrose	36	19	2	15	75	65	+10	40
8	Cowdenbeath	36	17	6	13	71	65	+6	40
9	Berwick Rangers	36	14	9	13	62	69	−7	37
10	Dumbarton	36	15	5	16	78	82	−4	35
11	Alloa Athletic	36	13	7	16	78	68	+10	33
12	Arbroath	36	13	7	16	56	76	−20	33
13	East Fife	36	14	4	18	70	80	−10	32
14	Brechin City	36	9	9	18	60	78	−18	27
15	Queen's Park	36	10	6	20	61	87	−26	26
16	East Stirlingshire	36	9	7	20	59	100	−41	25
17	Albion Rovers	36	9	6	21	60	89	−29	24
18	Forfar Athletic	36	10	4	22	65	98	−33	24
19	Morton	36	5	11	20	56	93	−37	21

1961 Five Nations Championship

The 1961 Five Nations Championship was the thirty-second series of the rugby union Five Nations Championship. Including the previous incarnations as the Home Nations and Five Nations, this was the sixty-seventh series of northern hemisphere rugby union championship. Ten matches were played between the 7th January and the 1 April. It was contested by England, France, Ireland, Scotland and Wales.

Table

Position	Nation	Games				Points			Table points
		Played	Won	Drawn	Lost	For	Against	Difference	
1	France	4	3	1	0	39	14	+25	7
2	Wales	4	2	0	2	21	14	+7	4
2	Scotland	4	2	0	2	19	25	−6	4
4	England	4	1	1	2	22	22	0	3
5	Ireland	4	1	0	3	22	48	−26	2

Results

France	11–0	Scotland
Wales	6–3	England
Ireland	11–8	England
Scotland	3–0	Wales
England	5–5	France
Scotland	16–8	Ireland
Wales	9–0	Ireland
England	6–0	Scotland
France	8–6	Wales
Ireland	3–15	France

Nation	Venue	City	Captain
England	Twickenham	London	Dickie Jeeps
France	Stade Olympique Yves-du-Manoir	Colombes	François Moncla
Ireland	Lansdowne Road	Dublin	Ronnie Dawson
Scotland	Murrayfield	Edinburgh	Gordon Waddell/Arthur Smith
Wales	National Stadium/St. Helens	Cardiff/Swansea	Terry Davies/Onllwyn Brace

The Masters 1961

e 1961 Masters Tournament was the 25th Masters Tournament, held
ril 6–10 at Augusta National Golf Club in Augusta, Georgia. Due to heavy
ns and flooding of several greens, Sunday's final round was halted before
.m. and the scores were erased, even though ten players had completed
ir rounds. Third round leader Gary Player was even par through eleven
es, and defending champion Arnold Palmer was two-under through
e. The entire round was replayed the next day. In the final round on
nday, Player defeated Palmer and amateur Charles Coe by one stroke to
come the first international champion at the Masters. Player made an up
d down from the bunker on the final hole but thought he had lost the
rnament, after carding a disappointing 40 (+4) on the back nine.

he final pairing with a one-shot lead, Palmer needed a par on the final hole for the win. From the fairway, his
roach shot also landed in the bunker right of the green. With a poor lie, Palmer's bunker shot went past the
e and off the green and down a hillock. Using his putter from off the green, he failed to get the fourth shot
se, and then missed the 15-foot (4.5 m) bogey putt which would have forced a playoff. It was the first of three
en jackets for Player, age 25, and the second of his nine major titles. His other wins at Augusta came over a
ade later in 1974 and 1978. Jack Nicklaus, 21, recorded the first of his 22 top-10 finishes at the Masters, his
 as an amateur. He tied for seventh, but the low amateur honours went to Coe. Nicklaus regained the U.S.
ateur title in September at Pebble Beach and turned professional in November.

Place	Player	Country	Score	To par	Money ($)
1	**Gary Player**	South Africa	69-68-69-74=280	−8	20,000
T2	Charles Coe (a)	United States	72-71-69-69=281	−7	0
	Arnold Palmer	United States	68-69-73-71=281		12,000
T4	Tommy Bolt	United States	72-71-74-68=285	−3	7,000
	Don January	United States	74-68-72-71=285		
6	Paul Harney	United States	71-73-68-74=286	−2	4,800
T7	Jack Burke, Jr.	United States	76-70-68-73=287	−1	3,200
	Billy Casper	United States	72-77-69-69=287		
	Bill Collins	United States	74-72-67-74=287		
	Jack Nicklaus (a)	United States	70-75-70-72=287		0

usta National Golf Club, sometimes referred to as Augusta or the National, is one of the most famous and
usive golf clubs in the world, located in Augusta, Georgia, United States. Unlike most private clubs which
rate as non-profits, Augusta National is a for-profit corporation, and it does not disclose its income, holdings,
nbership list, or ticket sales. Founded by Bobby Jones and Clifford Roberts, the course was designed by Jones
 Alister Mackenzie and opened for play in 1932. Since 1934, the club has played host to the annual Masters
rnament, one of the four major championships in professional golf, and the only major played each year at the
e course. It was the top-ranked course in Golf Digest's 2009 list of America's 100 greatest courses and was the
ber ten-ranked course based on course architecture on Golf week Magazine's 2011 list of best classic courses
e United States.

Grand National 1961

The 1961 Grand National was the 115th renewal of the world-famous Grand National horse race that took place at Aintree Racecourse near Liverpool, England, on the 25th March 1961. The winner was 28/1 shot Nicolaus Silver who became the first grey winner for 90 years. He was ridden by jockey Bobby Beasley and trained by Fred Rimell. In second place was last year's winner Merryman II. O'Malley Point finished third, whilst Scottish Flight was fourth. The favourite, Jonjo, finished 7th. Nicolaus Silver, a grey horse was bred in Tipperary, Ireland, by James Heffernan.

At that time, Nicolaus Silver was only the second grey horse to win the Aintree Grand National since its first running in 1839. There was not another grey winner until Neptune Collonge won the race in 2012.

Triple Crown Winners 1961

2,000 Guineas

Rockavon was a British Thoroughbred racehorse and sire, best known for winning the classic 2000 Guineas in 1961. After winning three races on minor tracks as a two-year-old and being well-beaten on his three-year-old debut Rockavon created a 66/1 upset when winning the 2000 Guineas, becoming the first horse trained in Scotland to win a classic. He subsequently only won one minor race and has been regarded as one of the least distinguished of classic winners. At the end of 1961 he was retired to stud where he made no impact as a sire winners.

St Leger

Aurelius was an Irish Thoroughbred racehorse and sire best known for winning the classic St Leger Stakes in 1 and for becoming one of the few classic winners to compete in steeplechases. As a two-year-old he finished fourth in his only appearance but was one of the best colts in Britain in the following year, winning the Craver Stakes and the King Edward VII Stakes before taking the St Leger. He was even better in 1962 when he won th Hardwicke Stakes and was narrowly beaten in the King George VI and Queen Elizabeth Stakes. He was retired stud but had serious fertility problems and later returned to the racecourse where he had a reasonably succes career in National Hunt racing.

The Derby

Psidium was an Irish-bred, British-trained Thoroughbred racehorse and sire. In a racing career that lasted fror 1960 to 1961 Psidium ran eleven times and won twice. At Epsom, Psidium was ridden by the French jockey Rc Poincelet. He was not considered a serious contender, starting at odds of 66/1 in a field of twenty-eight. The was run on rock-hard ground in front of a crowd estimated at 250,000 which included the Queen and the Que Mother. Psidium was held up towards the back of the field, and was not in contention when the leaders turne into the straight. In the final quarter of a mile, Poincelet moved Psidium to the wide outside and the colt produced a sudden burst of acceleration to move past the field.

1961 British Grand Prix

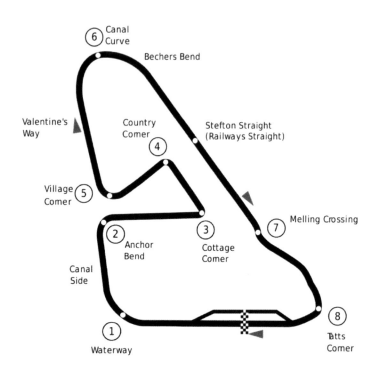

he 1961 British Grand Prix was a Formula One
otor race, held on the 15th July 1961 at the
ntree Circuit, near Liverpool. It was race 5 of 8
both the 1961 World Championship of Drivers
d the 1961 International Cup for Formula One
anufacturers.

llowing a wet weekend, with torrential rain
fecting both qualifying and the race start, the
and Prix was ultimately dominated by Scuderia
rrari, with their drivers taking all three podium
sitions. The race was won by German Wolfgang
n Trips, who had led for much of the race after
arting from fourth place on the grid.

is was von Trips's second but also his final
and Prix victory as two races later he was killed
an accident during the 1961 Italian Grand Prix.

Final Placings

Pos	No	Driver	Constructor	Laps	Time/Retired	Grid	Points
1	4	Wolfgang von Trips	Ferrari	75	2:40:53.6	4	9
2	2	Phil Hill	Ferrari	75	+46.0 secs	1	6
3	6	Richie Ginther	Ferrari	75	+46.8 secs	2	4
4	12	Jack Brabham	Cooper-Climax	75	+1:08.6	9	3
5	8	Jo Bonnier	Porsche	75	+1:16.2	3	2
6	36	Roy Salvadori	Cooper-Climax	75	+1:26.2	13	1
7	10	Dan Gurney	Porsche	74	+1 Lap	12	
8	14	Bruce McLaren	Cooper-Climax	74	+1 Lap	14	
9	22	Tony Brooks	BRM-Climax	73	+2 Laps	6	
10	16	Innes Ireland	Lotus-Climax	72	+3 Laps	7	

position winner Phil Hill drove to second place, on his way to winning the World Drivers' Championship at
end of the season, and third place was taken by Hill's American compatriot Richie Ginther.
1961 British Grand Prix is also notable as being the first occasion on which a four-wheel drive car and the last
hich a front engine car was entered for a World Championship race. These two accomplishments were
eved by the same vehicle: the experimental Ferguson P99-Climax run by the Rob Walker Racing Team.
ough the car was disqualified for receiving assistance on the track, in the hands of Stirling Moss – who took
r the car from first driver Jack Fairman after his own Lotus's brakes failed – it showed some promise. The 1961
sh Grand Prix also marked the last occasion on which Moss contested a Grand Prix race on home soil, as his
er was ended by an accident during a non-championship race prior to the 1962 season.

1961 Wimbledon Championships

The 1961 Wimbledon Championships took place on the outdoor grass courts at the All England Lawn Tennis and Croquet Club in Wimbledon, London, United Kingdom. The tournament ran from the 26th June until the 8th July. It was the 75th staging of the Wimbledon Championships, and the third Grand Slam tennis event of 1961.

Men's Singles

Rod Laver defeated Chuck McKinley in the final, 6–3, 6–1, 6–4 to win the Gentlemen's Singles tennis title at the 1961 Wimbledon Championships. Neale Fraser was the defending champion, but lost in the fourth round to Bobby Wilson.

Women's Singles

Angela Mortimer defeated Christine Truman in the final, 4–6, 6–4, 7–5 to win the Ladies' Singles tennis title at the 1961 Wimbledon Championships. It was the last all-British final to date. Maria Bueno was the defending champion, but did not defend her title due to jaundice.

Men's Doubles

Rafael Osuna and Dennis Ralston were the defending champions, but Osuna did not compete. Ralston competed with Chuck McKinley but lost in the quarterfinals to Roy Emerson and Neale Fraser.
Emerson and Fraser defeated Bob Hewitt and Fred Stolle in the final, 6–4, 6–8, 6–4, 6–8, 8–6 to win the Gentlemen' Doubles tennis title at the 1961 Wimbledon Championship.

Women's Doubles

Maria Bueno and Darlene Hard were the defending champions, but did not compete.
Karen Hantze and Billie Jean Moffitt defeated Jan Lehane and Margaret Smith in the final, 6–3, 6–4 to win the Ladies' Doubles tennis title at the 1961 Wimbledon Championships.

Mixed Doubles

Rod Laver and Darlene Hard were the defending champions, but did not compete.
Fred Stolle and Lesley Turner defeated Bob Howe and Edda Buding in the final, 11–9, 6–2 to win the Mixed Doubles tennis title at the 1961 Wimbledon Championships.

Rod Laver

Angela Mortimer

Pale Horse is a work of detective fiction by Agatha Christie and
t published in the UK by the Collins Crime Club on the 6th
vember 1961. Mark Easterbrook, the hero of the book and its
ncipal narrator, sees a fight between two girls in a Chelsea coffee
during which one pulls out some of the other's hair at the roots.
n afterwards he learns that this second girl, Thomasina
kerton, has died. At dinner with a friend, a woman named Poppy
ling mentions something called the Pale Horse that arranges
ths, but is suddenly scared at having mentioned it and will say no
re.

en Mark goes to Much Deeping with the famous mystery writer,
dne Oliver, to a village fete organised by his cousin, he learns of
ouse converted from an old inn called the Pale Horse, now
abited by three modern "witches" led by Thyrza Grey. Visiting
ses in the area, he meets a wheelchair-using man, Mr Venables,
 has no apparent explanation for his substantial wealth. At the
 of the novel it is revealed that Osborne has been the brains
ind the Pale Horse organisation; the black magic element was
rely a piece of misdirection on his part, while the murders were
ly committed by replacing products the victims had named in the
 survey with poisoned ones.

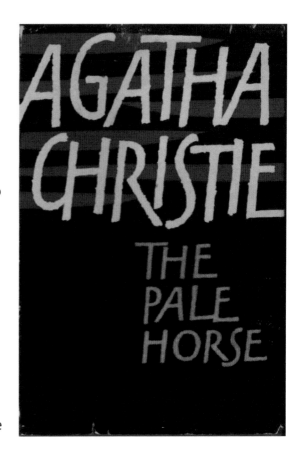

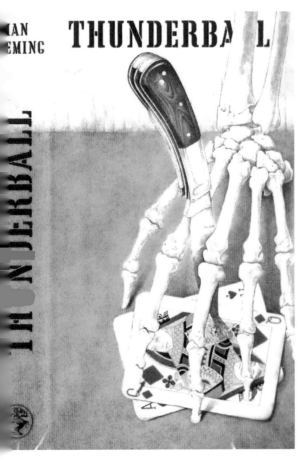

Thunderball is the ninth book in Ian Fleming's James Bond
series, and the eighth full-length Bond novel. It was first
published in the UK by Jonathan Cape on the 27th March 1961,
where the initial print run of 50,938 copies quickly sold out.
The story centres on the theft of two atomic bombs by the
crime syndicate SPECTRE and the subsequent attempted
blackmail of the Western powers for their return. James Bond,
Secret Service operative 007, travels to the Bahamas to work
with his friend Felix Leiter, seconded back into the CIA for the
investigation. Thunderball also introduces SPECTRE's leader
Ernst Stavro Blofeld, in the first of three appearances in Bond
novels, with On Her Majesty's Secret Service and You Only
Live Twice being the others. In 1965, the film Thunderball was
released, starring Sean Connery as James Bond. The film was
produced as the fourth Eon Productions film and, as well as
listing Albert R. Broccoli and Harry Saltzman as producers,
Kevin McClory was also included in the production team:
Broccoli and Saltzman made a deal with McClory, to
undertake a joint production of Thunderball, which stopped
McClory from making any further version of the novel for a
period of ten years following the release of the Eon-produced
version. Thunderball premiered in Tokyo on the 9th December
1965, grossing $141.2 million at the global box office.

The Fox in the Attic is a 1961 novel by Richard Hughes, who is best known for A High Wind in Jamaica. It was the first novel in his unfinished The Human Predicament trilogy. The novel opens in 1923. The protagonist, a young Welsh aristocrat named Augustine Penry-Herbert, discovers the body of a young girl and is incorrectly suspected of having something to do with her accidental death. Augustine decides to leave England and visit distant relations in Germany. He falls in love with his cousin Mitzi amidst the rise of Nazism, including the Munich Putsch. At the end of the novel, Mitzi, who has lost her sight, enters a convent and Augustine returns to England. The Fox in the Attic was originally published in 1961 by Chatto & Windus: London as v. 1 of The Human Predicament trilogy, and then in the United States by Harper & Brothers: New York. This was 23 years after Hughes's previous novel, In Hazard: A Sea Story, and 33 years after A High Wind in Jamaica, which was a best seller in the United Kingdom and America.

The Fox in the Attic was featured in the 2nd February 1962 Life Guide section of Life Magazine. In this short blurb, Life introduced Hughes's attempt to write The Human Predicament trilogy, calling it a "vast, Tolstoyan novel sequence" while also saying of the first volume, "Hughes effectively interweaves the life of his hero...with the fortunes of top Nazidom."

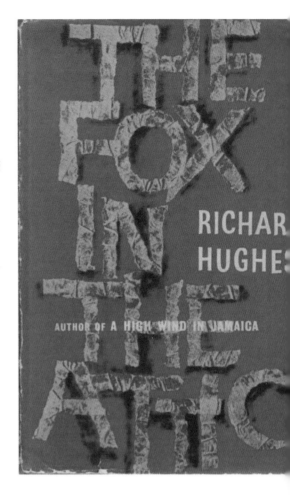

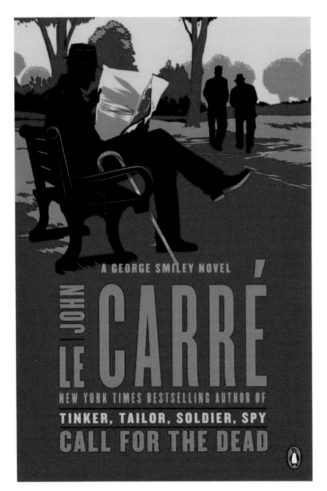

Call for the Dead is John le Carré's first novel, published in 1961. It introduces George Smiley, the most famous of le Carré's recurring characters, in a story about East German s[?] inside Great Britain. It also introduces a fictional version of British Intelligence, called "the Circus" because of its locatio[n] Cambridge Circus, that is apparently based on MI6 and that recurs throughout le Carré's spy novels. Call for the Dead w[as] filmed as The Deadly Affair, released in 1966.

Foreign Office civil servant Samuel Fennan apparently comm[its] suicide after a routine security check by Circus agent Georg[e] Smiley. Smiley had interviewed and cleared Fennan only da[ys] previously after an anonymous accusation; because of this, Circus head of service Maston sets up Smiley to be blamed [for] Fennan's death. While interviewing Fennan's wife Elsa in he[r] home, Smiley answers the telephone, expecting the call to [be] for him. It is a requested 8:30 AM call from the telephone exchange. Inspector Mendel, a police officer on the verge o[f] retirement who is investigating the Fennan case, finds out t[hat] the call had been requested by Fennan the night before. W[hen] Elsa later tells Smiley that she requested the call from the exchange, Smiley becomes suspicious of her. However, Ma[ston] unequivocally orders Smiley to refrain from any further investigation into Fennan's death.

Severed Head is a satirical, sometimes farcical 1961 novel by Iris Murdoch. It was Murdoch's fifth published novel.

Martin Lynch-Gibbon is a well-to-do 41-year-old wine merchant whose childless marriage to an older woman called Antonia has been one of convenience rather than love. It never occurs to him that his ongoing secret affair with Georgie, a young academic in her twenties, could be immoral. Martin is shocked when his wife tells him that she has been having an affair with Palmer Anderson, her psychoanalyst and a friend of the couple. Antonia informs Martin that she wants to divorce him and marry Anderson.

Martin moves out of their London house in Hereford Square. Before officially moving, Martin visits his brother Alexander's home near Oxford. While there he learns that Antonia has already written to Alexander about the divorce, leaving Alexander quite shaken. Later Martin returns to Hereford Square, where Antonia, now acting as a mother figure for him, tries to set up his new accommodation. After arguing with Antonia, he goes to the station to pick up Palmer's half-sister Honor Klein, a lecturer in anthropology who is visiting from Cambridge.

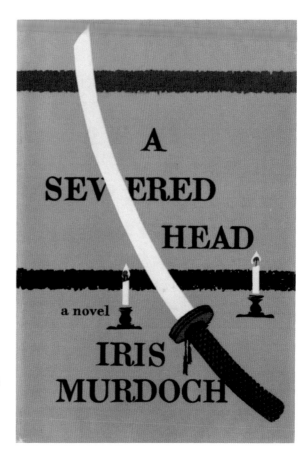

The Prime of Miss Jean Brodie is a novel by Muriel Spark, the best known of her works. It first saw publication in The New Yorker magazine and was published as a book by Macmillan in 1961. The character of Miss Jean Brodie brought Spark international fame and brought her into the first rank of contemporary Scottish literature.

In 1930s Edinburgh, six ten-year-old girls, Sandy, Rose, Mary, Jenny, Monica, and Eunice are assigned Miss Jean Brodie, who describes herself as being "in my prime," as their teacher. Miss Brodie, determined that they shall receive an education in the original sense of the Latin verb educere, "to lead out," gives her students lessons about her personal love life and travels, promoting art history, classical studies, and fascism. Under her mentorship, these six girls whom Brodie singles out as the elite group among her students—known as the "Brodie set"—begin to stand out from the rest of the school. However, in one of the novel's typical flash-forwards we learn that one of them will later betray Brodie, ruining her teaching career, but that she will never learn which one. In the Junior School, they meet the singing teacher, the short Mr Gordon Lowther, and the art master, the handsome, one-armed war veteran Mr Teddy Lloyd, a married Roman Catholic with six children. These two teachers form a love triangle with Miss Brodie, each loving her, while she loves only Mr Lloyd.

West Side Story is the award-winning adaptation of the classic romantic tragedy "Romeo and Juliet". The feuding families become two warring New York City gangs--the white Jets led by Riff and the Latino Sharks, led by Bernardo. Their hatred escalates to a point where neither can coexist with any form of understanding. But whe Riff's best friend (and former Jet) Tony and Bernardo's younger sist Maria meet at a dance, no one can do anything to stop their love. Maria and Tony begin meeting in secret, planning to run away. The the Sharks and Jets plan a rumble under the highway--whoever win gains control of the streets. Maria sends Tony to stop it, hoping it can end the violence. It goes terribly wrong, and before the lovers know what's happened, tragedy strikes and doesn't stop until the climactic and heart-breaking ending.

Winner of 10 Academy Awards including Best Picture and Best Sound.

Box office $44,055,492

Run time is 2h 33mins

Trivia

When filming "The Taunting Scene", Rita Moreno was reduced to tears when she was harassed and nearly raped by the Jets, as it brought back memories of when she was raped as a child. When she started crying, th Jets immediately stopped what they were doing and tried to comfort her, while pointing out that the audien was going to hate them for what they were doing.

The actors in the rival gangs were instructed to play pranks on each other off the set to keep tensions high.

During the entire production, the actors wore out 200 pairs of shoes, applied more than 100lbs of make-up, split 27 pairs of pants and performed in 30 different recording sessions.

Goofs

There are several instances of gang members (most notably the Jets) mouthing the wrong words during the songs.

In the opening number, which was shot on location in NYC, the playground is easily 300 feet x 300 feet in siz Later on, when it is obvious they were on the studio back lot, the playground has shrunk to around 30 feet b 30 feet.

After the war council, Schrank says that he rebuked the Jets the same day. That means that all events before the war council were on that day too. The dance started at 10 PM, and that leaves very little time for the "America" song, the balcony scene and the war council.

In the final scene, they show Maria, and then pan over to the Jets and Sharks. When they come back to Mar a large portion of her hair has magically come out of place.

The Parent Trap. Thirteen-year-olds prim and proper Bostonian Sharon McKendrick and tomboyish Californian Susan Evers meet at summer camp. It's hate at first sight, as besides the differing length of their hair, they look exactly the same. After the girls carry out one battle after another against each other, the camp administrators ultimately place the two in solitary confinement, the two eating, sleeping, and playing only with each other. It is during this confinement that they finally get a chance to know each other and learn that they are indeed twins, separated when they were babies when their parents, Maggie McKendrick and Mitch Evers, divorced. Wanting to get to know and ultimately love the parent they never met, Sharon and Susan decide to switch places, Sharon will go to California and pretend to be Susan, and Susan will go to Boston and pretend to be Sharon. The other thing they believe is that their parents still love each other, why else had neither ever remarried.

Nominated for 2 Oscars

Box office $29,650,385

Run time 2h 09mins

⌐ia

⌐ne dance party scene, where the layer cake falls off the beak of the totem pole and drops onto Miss Inch's ⌐th McDevitt's) face, director David Swift originally wanted to cut the shot of the cake-fall. But when Walt ⌐ney saw the rushes, he told Swift to leave the shot in, saying it would be the biggest laugh in the movie. Turns ⌐ Walt was right.

⌐ screenplay originally called for only a few trick photography shots of Hayley Mills in scenes with herself. The ⌐ of the movie was to be shot using a body double. When Walt Disney saw how seamless the processed shots ⌐e, he ordered the script reconfigured to include more of the visual effect.

⌐ina Barnes (Vicky) is the only actress to also appear in the 1998 remake. She plays an older version of her ⌐acter, which has passed her gold digging ways on to her daughter Meredith.

⌐fs

⌐n after Sharon arrives at Susan's home (pretending to be Susan), Verbena says something about washing all of ⌐n's dirty camp clothes, but is seen putting many of them directly into the dressers in Susan's room without ⌐hing them first.

⌐r the fight at the dance, a shot shows Sharon and Susan on the ground, covered in food. Susan's dress, which ⌐on had cut the back out with scissors earlier, is brand new, as if it had never been cut.

⌐y is tricked into going on the camping trip at the last minute, with no time to pack any bags or gear. Yet when ⌐ get to the campsite, she has curlers to wear to bed.

⌐e isolation cabin, when the window blows open and the girls try to close it, the stand-in's face is revealed.

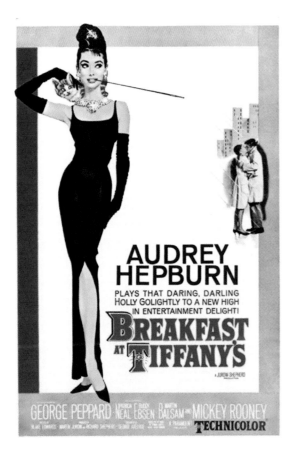

Breakfast at Tiffany's. After one of her frequent visits to Tiffany's--New York City's dazzling jewellery store--and the maximum securit Sing-Sing prison for mobster Sally Tomato's weekly "weather report", Holly Golightly, Manhattan's elegant socialite, finds herse infatuated with her charming new neighbour, Paul Varjak. Stuck ir persistent creative rut, Paul, too, lets himself drawn into Holly's superficial world, of course, not because he likes the idea that he reminds her of her brother, but because, little by little, he succum to Holly's beguiling allure. Even though they don't openly admit it, the two reluctant lovers have a past that they struggle to keep at bay; nevertheless, are their well-hidden secrets powerful enough keep them apart? After all, Paul and Holly are meant for each oth Will an early-morning breakfast at Tiffany's be the prelude to a breezy young love?

Box Office: Budget $2.,500,000

Oscar Winner: Best Music & Scoring of a Musical Picture

Run time 1h 55mins.

Trivia

Although not visible on camera, hundreds of onlookers watched Audrey Hepburn's window-shopping scene at the start of the film. This made her nervous and she kept making mistakes. It wasn't until a crew member nearly got electrocuted behind the camera that she pulled herself together and finished the scene.

At a post-production meeting following a screening of the film, a studio executive, in reference to "Moon River," said, "Well, I think the first thing we can do is get rid of that stupid song." Audrey Hepburn stood up at the table and said, "Over my dead body!" The song stayed in the picture.

Tiffany's opened its doors on a Sunday for the first time since the 19th century so that filming could take place inside the store.

Goofs

When Holly first looks through Paul's window and sees the 'decorator' leaving him $300 while he sleeps, the ornate gold clock in the background reads 11:30. However just a few minutes later, once Holly is inside the room, we see it again and it now clearly shows 4:30. For the next five minutes, it remains on 4:30, without moving at all.

When Holly sneaks into Paul's apartment to visit the night after they first meet, he is wearing a watch on his right wrist. However, when he states, "They bought what's in that box," while pointing to a box filled with copies of his novel, the watch disappears. It reappears in the next shot.

Paul's apartment is clearly on the third floor as we know from all the scenes early in the film and yet when Pa returns home with groceries he unlocks his apartment on the first floor.

ONE GREAT BIG ONEDERFUL MOTION PICTURE

WALT DISNEY'S NEW ALL-CARTOON FEATURE

One Hundred and One Dalmatians

technicolor

101 Dalmatians. Pongo is a male Dalmatian living in London with his master, Roger, a bachelor songwriter who has yet to sell his first tune. Bored with their single existence, Pongo arranges for Roger to meet Anita, a pretty young woman who just happens to have a female Dalmatian named Perdita. It is not long before love blossoms all around and a double wedding takes place. A few months later, Perdita gives birth to 15 puppies, much to the delight of Cruella De Vil, a wealthy, wicked former schoolmate of Anita's whose burning passion is to own a coat made of Dalmatian pelts. When she is unable to purchase the puppies, she has them "dognapped" and brought to her crumbling estate in the country, where 84 other Dalmatians are also being held captive. All attempts by the police to find the missing pups fail, and the desperate Pongo and Perdita appeal to the dogs of London, via the "twilight bark." Led by The Colonel, an indomitable shaggy dog and a cat named Sergeant Tibbs, all dogdom comes to the rescue and, aided by geese, cows, and horses, tracks down the missing puppies.

Box Office: Gross worldwide $216,026,182

Run time 1h 19mins

via

[th]e birth of the puppies actually happened to the author Dodie Smith. Her Dalmatians had 15 puppies, one was [bor]n lifeless and her husband revived it. However, they sold most of them, and kept only a small number.

[th]e company was in debt following the flop of Sleeping Beauty (1959) and desperately needed a hit. There was [eve]n talk of closing down the animation division as the company was refocusing on live action films, television [and] theme parks.

[the] author of the book on which the film is based, Dodie Smith, was a successful playwright and novelist who [had] nine Dalmatians of her own, including one named Pongo. She got the idea for the book when a friend who [was] at her house saw all the dogs together and remarked, "Those dogs would make a lovely fur coat."

[Go]ofs

[Pat]ch's right ear is solid black, and his left ear spotted. However, sometimes the left ear is solid white, and [som]etimes it's solid black. In the same scene where Patch turns into Lucky, his ear goes from spotted to white, [and] in the following scene in the Colonel's barn, both of his ears are solid black.

[Wh]en Perdita and Pongo are nuzzling after the news that Cruella is not going to get any of their puppies, before [it c]hanges to the scene to reveal the puppies nursing, the tags on Perdita and Pongo's collars vanish.

[Wh]en Pongo pulls Roger and Anita into the pond Perdita remains on land. Yet when Roger is helping Anita out, [Per]dita walks out of the pond and Pongo, next to her is shown to be perfectly dry.

Judgement at Nuremberg. It's 1948 in Nuremberg, Germany, where the American military is holding a post-WWII tribunal o the activities of individuals within the Nazi Party leading up to and during the war. Dan Haywood is the lead judge in a three-man judiciary in one of those trials, where four men, who wer involved in judicial matters, are the defendants. The general issues surrounding these four is whether they are guilty of international crimes or were just carrying out the laws of their national government, especially as they did not run or operate concentration camps for example, or purportedly know about what was happening to anyone they sentenced to life at those concentration camps. Of the four on trial, the largest question mark surrounds Dr. Ernst Janning, a globally renowned judge. Haywood, not being a well-travelled man outside of the US, tries to get to know life in Germany, both then and now, to ge a better perspective of the discussions at the trial. He befrienc a Mrs. Bertholt as that conduit into German life.

Box Office Budget: $3,000,000 (estimated)

Winner of 2 Oscars, Best Actor & Best Writing

Run time 2h 59mins

Trivia

Marlon Brando wanted to play the role of Hans Rolfe, the German lawyer who defends the German judges. Brando, in a rare attempt to garner the part, actually approached Director Stanley Kramer about it. Although Kramer and Screenwriter Abby Mann were very intrigued with the idea of having an actor of Brando's talent an stature in the role, both were so impressed with Maximilian Schell's portrayal of the same part in the original television broadcast Playhouse 90: Judgment at Nuremberg (1959), that they had decided to stick with the relatively unknown Schell, who later won the Oscar for Best Actor for that role.

Watching Maximilian Schell shoot a scene one day, Spencer Tracy said to Richard Widmark, "We've got to watc out for that young man. He's very good. He's going to walk away with the Oscar for this picture." This is exactly what happened.

Goofs

The housekeeper, Mrs. Halbestadt, says that Mrs. Bertholt's husband was executed in connection with the Malmedy massacre during the Battle of the Bulge. Although many Germans were found guilty for the massacre and some were sentenced to death, none of them was ever actually executed.

None of the American officers have shoulder patches on their coats. As a minimum, they all should be wearing the insignia of their current organization on their left sleeve. In addition, officers with World War II service shou have the patch of their previous unit on their right sleeve.

In an outdoor scene, several US Army MPs are shown in the background standing at parade rest with rifles. Instead of being armed with the standard issued rifle of the day, US M-1 Garand's, the guards are holding Britis Lee-Enfield's, which were used in WWI and WWII by the British Army.

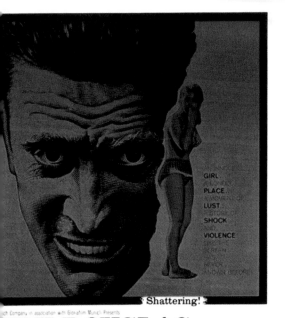

Town Without Pity. In 1960 Germany, Army lawyer Major Steve Garrett is assigned to defend four American soldiers charged with raping 16 year-old Karin Steinhof. She was swimming in a nearby river when the four of them came across her and they were soon arrested thereafter. Maj. Garrett is anything but impressed with his clients but his job is to give them the best defence possible. He tries to obtain a plea bargain but Karin's father flatly refuses and the prosecutor, Colonel Jerome Pakenham, is seeking the death penalty. In order for the death penalty to be applied, the defence attorney must have the opportunity to thoroughly examine the victim under oath. He sympathizes with Karin and does his best to convince Karin father to keep her from testifying. When he refuses, Garrett is left will little choice but to attack her on the stand.

Winner of 2 Golden Globes
Best Music, Original Song. Dimitri Tiomkin (music) Ned Washington (lyrics) For the song "Town Without Pity"

Most Promising Newcomer - Female - Christine Kaufmann

Run time 1h 45mins

...ia

...stine Kaufmann was actually 16 years old when she played the 16 year old rape victim in this movie.

...ough Christine Kaufmann receives an "introducing" credit, she had appeared in several credited roles in ...ure films beginning in 1953.

...or Garrett is first seen driving into town in a 1956 Chevrolet Bel Air convertible coupe. He drives through ...Nuremberg gate of the Forchheim Fortress in Upper Franconia, Bavaria.

...left shoulder patch seen on most of the uniforms indicates the U.S. 7th Army.

...on Trumbo (from his autobiography) helped out Kirk Douglas by contributing to the script.

...fs

...e near end, when Kirk Douglas is checking out of the hotel, through the double glass doors is clearly visible ...57 Chevrolet rear 1/4 panel with its fluted aluminium trim. Camera change to the exterior of the hotel, Kirk ...las exits and walks around to the driver's side of a 1956 Chevrolet which he drives away in.

...n Maj. Garrett is first interviewing Cpl Scott, as Garrett is walking back towards Scott, a moving shadow of ...oom microphone is visible upper left of the frame.

...k swims across the river to be with Karin. However, when he is standing by her, his swim trunks are ...ally wet and partially dry.

The Innocents. In late nineteenth century England, Miss Giddens (Deborah Kerr) becomes governess of a small orph[a] girl living in a lonely stately home occupied only by the child[ ] housekeeper, and a small complement of servants. Her init[ia] misgivings allayed by the child's angelic nature, her anxietie[s] are once more aroused when the girl's brother, equally captivating, is sent home from boarding school for wickedn[ess] of some unspecified kind. Eerie apparitions and inexplicable behaviour on the children's part cause her to wonder about the house's history, especially about the fate of the previou[s] governess, Miss Jessel (Clytie Jessop), and the former valet, Peter Quint (Peter Wyngarde). She fears for the children's souls and for her own sanity. Eventually convinced that ther[e] an unnatural force at work, perverting the innocence of her charges, she sets out to secure the children's salvation by wresting them from its power. Though her struggle reaches[ ] resolution, its real nature and its outcome ultimately remai[n] ambiguous.

Nominated for 2 BAFTAS

Run time 1h 40mins

Trivia

Producer and Director Jack Clayton didn't want the children to be exposed to the darker themes of the story, [so] they never saw the screenplay in its entirety. The children were given their pages the day before they were to [be] filmed.

Twentieth Century Fox executives were highly nervous about the admittedly unsettling scene where the governess kisses the boy Miles directly on his lips.

Second-billed (for contractual requirements) Peter Wyngarde does not have a single line of dialogue, and only[ ] appears in the movie in a handful of short scenes that total far less than one minute's running time.

Kate Bush was inspired by this movie to pen the song "The Infant Kiss" which appears on her 1980 album "Ne[ver] For Ever".

Goofs

An obvious center back zipper in several of Miss Kerr's costumes, as well as in Mrs. Gross & Flora's costumes. [The] Innocents is set during the Victorian period, 1837-1901. Commercial zippers were not used in clothing until 1[9..]

At the beginning of the film, when The Uncle walks from behind his desk over to the fireplace in his office, a moving shadow of the boom microphone is visible upper left of the frame.

Miss Giddens is wearing one dress when Flora bursts in to tell them to come see Miles riding the horse. Whe[n] they run outside, Miss Giddens is wearing a different dress.

GLENN **FORD** BETTE **DAVIS** HOPE **LANGE** ARTHUR **O'CONNELL**

PETER **FALK** THOMAS **MITCHELL** EDWARD EVERETT **HORTON** MICKEY **SHAUGHNESSY**

Pocketful Of Miracles. Boozy, brassy Apple Annie, a beggar with a basket of apples, is as much as part of downtown New York City as old Broadway itself. Bootlegger Dave the Dude is a sucker for her apples, he thinks they bring him luck. But Dave and girlfriend Queenie Martin need a lot more than luck when it turns out that Annie is in a jam and only they can help. Annie's daughter Louise, who has lived all her life in a Spanish convent, is coming to America with a Count and his son.

The Count's son wants to marry Louise, who thinks her mother is part of New York City society. It's up to Dave and Queenie and their Runyonesque cronies to turn Annie into a lady and convince the Count and his son that they are hobnobbing with New York City's elite.

Golden Globe winner
Best Actor - Comedy or Musical Glenn Ford and
Most Promising Newcomer – Female – Ann Margret.

Run time 2h 16mins

via

ording to the Bette Davis biography, "Fasten Your Seatbelts", the actress was furious when she read a Glenn d interview in which the actor claimed to have gotten her the part because of the boost she had given him rs before in A Stolen Life (1946). Davis is quoted as saying, "Who is that son of a bitch that he should say he ped me have a comeback! That shitheel wouldn't have helped me out of a sewer!"

ector Frank Capra wanted Dean Martin or Frank Sinatra to play Dave, and Shirley Jones for Queenie. After the dio turned down Capra's alternate choice Steve McQueen, Glenn Ford was cast as Dave and helped finance film through his production company, he asked for his girlfriend Hope Lange as Queenie.

te Davis got furious with Glenn Ford when he asked her to give up the star's dressing room next to his so his friend Hope Lange could have it. Davis absolutely refused.

ofs

ing the police escort to the boat in the last few minutes of the movie, a 1949 Cadillac can be seen in the rear dow of the car the governor is riding in on the right side of his head. The movie is set in 1930's

en Dave demands $100,000 from Darcey, he is shaking his fist while holding an apple. The camera cuts to ther angle, and Dave is shaking an empty fist.

r the fight at the dock Dave the Dude and Joy Boy are in the apartment waiting for Darcy to call. Dave is lying the couch throwing darts with his feet up. In the long shot a newspaper is resting flat under his feet but when wn closer up the newspaper is re-positioned lying against the back of the couch so the headline (FBI HINTS RCY IS IN NY) can be read.

20th Century-Fox presents
PAUL NEWMAN in ROBERT ROSSEN'S powerful Award-Winning drama **"THE HUSTLER"**
co-starring Piper Laurie · George C. Scott and **JACKIE GLEASON** as "Minnesota Fats"
with Myron McCormick · Produced and Directed by Robert Rossen · Screenplay by Sidney
Carrol and Robert Rossen · CINEMASCOPE

The Hustler. With his friend Charlie Burns, "Fast" Eddie Felson has long earned whatever money he has as a pool shark, he and Charlie traveling the country hustling new unsuspecting targets at each stop. Against Charlie's wishes, Eddie wants to give up his anonymity to prove that he is the best by taking on the best, namely Minnesota Fats whose home pool hall is the Ames in New York City. Eddie knows he's talented, but gambler Bert Gordon, who Eddie meets at the Ames and who can also see that Eddie is talented, believes that Eddie needs more than talent to beat Fats. Bert wants to take Eddie under his wing to finance Eddie's challenge, not only against Fats, but against all comers, in turn showing Eddie the character that he is inherently missing to be the best. The price? A seventy-five percent cut. As Eddie decides what to do with regard to Bert's proposal, Eddie begins a relationship with Sarah Packard, a woman who has as self-destructive tendencies as Eddie, she who is not averse to imbibing first thing in the morning. Being involved with Bert and Sarah may be incompatible in Eddie's current life, especially as Bert and Sarah see different things that Eddie needs for fulfilment, which do not include the other person.

Run time 2h 14mins

Trivia

Paul Newman and Jackie Gleason established a friendship on the set. At one point, Newman got a little cocky about his newfound pool skills and challenged the much more experienced Gleason to a $50 bet on a game. Newman broke, and then it was Gleason's turn. He knocked all 15 balls in and Newman never got another shot. Gleason recalled that the next day Newman paid him off with 5000 pennies.

All the pool shots in the movie are performed by the actors themselves (Paul Newman and Jackie Gleason) except one: the massé shot (cue ball sends two object balls into the same pocket), performed by Willie Mosconi.

Paul Newman had never held a pool cue before he landed the role of Fast Eddie Felson. He took out the dining room table from his home and installed a pool table so he could spend every waking hour practicing and polishing up his skills.

Goofs

During the last pool match, second game, Minnesota Fats has taken his jacket off, loosened his tie and unbuttoned his vest, but one subsequent shot shows him with his tie tightened and wearing a buttoned vest and jacket.

When Sarah writes words on the mirror, she writes "TWISTEd" - all capital letters except for the "d". When it is shown later, when Eddie is in the room, it is written in all lower case letters.

During the last game, Eddie calls and pockets the 1 ball. Then he sets up, calls the 12 ball and you hear the ball dropping into the pocket. Eddie then walks around to the other side of the table and calls the next shot - the 12 ball again.

The Misfits. Roslyn is a very beautiful woman who just got divorced. She meets two friends, Guido and Gay, who take her to Guido's house in the country to relax and forget the difficulties of the past few weeks. Everything is fine at first, but soon the two men fall in love with Roslyn and start showing some bad aspects of their characters. Soon they meet another friend of Gay's, and the four of them go to hunt some wild horses. This is when things just... explode!

Directors Guild of America nominee for Outstanding Directorial Achievement in Motion Pictures - John Huston

Genesis Award Winner - Feature Film – Classic

Run time 2h 05mins

via

the last day of filming, Clark Gable said regarding Marilyn Monroe, "Christ, I'm glad this picture's finished. She near gave me a heart attack." He was probably referring to her unexpectedly going nude during a bedroom ne. On the next day, Gable suffered a severe coronary thrombosis and died ten days later at age 59.

n Huston was often late to the set after spending all night gambling. Clark Gable took it all in stride. He was dy when called and simply waited with his script open to the page being shot that day. When someone asked ne lateness upset him, he said, "No, it doesn't drive me mad. Of course it would be better if we did start. But being paid for it, very handsomely."

rilyn Monroe blamed herself for Clark Gable's death. However it should be noted that Gable was already in or health when filming began. He had been a chain smoker since his mid-teens, and until recently he had been eavy drinker. Twice over the past decade he had suffered severe chest pains which could have been heart cks.

ofs

en the rodeo PA announcer introduces Perce Howland [Montgomery Clift] on a bucking horse, he says vland is from "White River, Wyoming." Howland corrects him with a shouted "California, not Wyoming." This forces Howland's remark at the pay phone that he was trying to call home but the operator kept giving him oming rather than California. When Howland later mounts a Brahma bull, the PA announcer says, "Perce vland of Black Hills, Colorado." Perce said he had recently been in Colorado, so the confusion of origins is erstandable and perhaps intentional.

en Monroe and Cliff are behind the bar sitting near an old car and a pile of beer cans, the cans change places n cut to cut when seen from behind Monroe down to Cliff.

en Gay is seeing Susan off at the train station she is supposed to be traveling east to St. Louis but the train she rds is heading west.

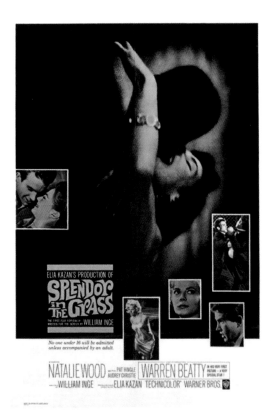

Splendour In Our Grass. It's 1928 in oil rich southeast Kansas. High school seniors Bud Stamper and Deanie Loomis are in love with each other. Bud, the popular football captain, and Deanie, the sensitive soul, are "good" kids who have only gone as far as kissing. Unspoken to each other, they expect to get married to each other one day. But both face pressures within the relationship, Bud who has the urges to go farther despite knowing in his heart that if they do that Deanie will end up with a reputation like his own sister, Ginny Stamper, known as the loose, immoral party girl, and Deanie who will do anything to hold onto Bud regardless of the consequences. They also face pressures from their parents who have their own expectation for their offspring. Bud's overbearing father, Ace Stamper, the local oil baron, does not believe Bud can do wrong and expects him to go to Yale after graduation, which does not fit within Bud's own expectations for himself. And the money and image conscious Mrs. Loomis just wants Deanie to get married as soon as possible to Bud so that Deanie will have a prosperous life in a rich family. When Bud makes a unilateral decision under these pressures, it leads to a path which affects both his and Deanie's future.

Run time 2h 04mins

Trivia

Depicts the first French kiss in a Hollywood film. It occurs between Warren Beatty (Bud) and Jan Norris (Juanita) during the waterfall scene.

Even though they were supposed to be playing teenagers, Natalie Wood and Warren Beatty were approximately 22 and 23 respectively at the time of filming. As a result, Elia Kazan decided that the other actors who were to play teenagers in the film should be in their early to mid-twenties as a way to make it easier for the audience to accept Wood and Beatty as teenagers rather than as adults playing teens.

According to one of the makeup artists, the crew found Warren Beatty arrogant and didn't like him. In fact, he was given the nickname "Mental Anguish" or "M.A." for short that crew members called him behind his back.

The very brief glimpse we get of a building in Yale is not Yale, but CCNY, the City College of New York.

Goofs

At the film's climax, when Hazel asks Deanie if she still loves Bud, you can see to the right of the frame that Deanie is wearing her hat. However, when it cuts immediately to a close-up of Deanie, she is not wearing the hat.

In a close up scene where Wilma Dean and Bud are kissing and talking outside Wilma Dean's house, you can see Wilma stepping down off some kind of box she was using so the two could be in frame.

During the bath tub scene, there is chunk of dry ice providing the "steam".

Although it is accepted as fact that many Wall Street investors jumped to their deaths after the crash of 1929, it all a myth. Although the suicide rate throughout the country did steadily increase during the years between 19. and 1932. The crash of 1929 was the beginning of the ten year period known as the Great Depression.

MUSIC 1961

Artist	Single	Reached number one	Weeks at number one
	1961		
iff Richard and The Shadows	I Love You	29th December 1960	2
ohnny Tillotson	Poetry in Motion	12th January 1961	2
vis Presley	Are You Lonesome Tonight?	26th January 1961	4
etula Clark	Sailor	23rd February 1961	1
e Everly Brothers	Walk Right Back	2nd March 1961	3
vis Presley	Wooden Heart	23rd March 1961	6
e Marcels	Blue Moon	4th May 1961	2
oyd Cramer	On the Rebound	18th May 1961	1
e Temperance Seven	You're Driving Me Crazy	25th May 1961	1
vis Presley	Surrender	1st June 1961	9
l Shannon	Runaway	29th June 1961	3
e Everly Brothers	Temptation	20th July 1961	2
en Kane	Well I Ask You	3rd August 1961	1
len Shapiro	You Don't Know	10th August 1961	3
hn Leyton	Johnny Remember Me	31st August 1961	3
irley Bassey	Reach for the Stars	21st September1961	1
hn Leyton	Johnny Remember Me	28th September 1961	1
e Shadows	Kon-Tiki	5th October 1961	1
chael	The Highwaymen	12th October 1961	1
len Shapiro	Walkin' Back to Happiness	19th October 1961	3
is Presley	Little Sister / His Latest Flame	9th November 1961	4
ankie Vaughan	Tower of Strength	7th December 1961	3
nny Williams	Moon River	28th December 1961	2

sically, the charts still reflected a wide range of tastes, with Shirley Bassey, Matt Monro, Frankie Vaughan and
y Stewart slugging it out with US acts such as Elvis, The Drifters, the Everly's and Bobby Vee. Jazz was well
esented with Acker Bilk, The Temperance Seven, Kenny Ball, Cleo Laine and Johnny Dankworth. The ever
ular Lonnie Donnegan was still knocking out the hits and Cliff Richard, Billy Fury and Adam Faith continued to
e female teenage hearts to flutter, while 14 year old singing sensation Helen Shapiro had two number 1
es. In the US, Motown had their first million selling single with "Shop Around" by The Miracles. It would be
ther six years before the name was changed to Smokey Robinson and the Miracles.

Cliff Richard and The Shadows

"I Love You"

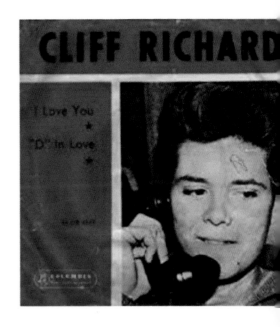

"I Love You" is the fourth UK number-one hit single (and the second of the 1960s) by Cliff Richard and the Shadows. It was written by the Shadows' rhythm guitarist Bruce Welch. Released in November 1960, it was a Christmas No. 1 and stayed at the chart summit for two weeks, although it did not carry a traditional holiday theme.

The B side was D' In Love.

It took until 1977 before another song entitled "I Love You" entered the UK Singles Chart. It was recorded by Donna Summer.

Johnny Tillotson

"Poetry in Motion"

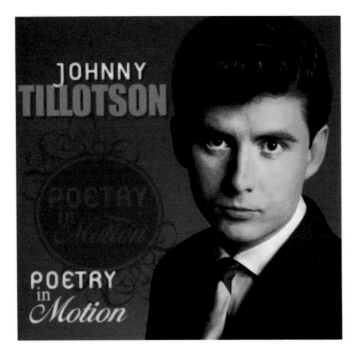

"Poetry in Motion" is a UK number-one hit single in 19 recorded amongst others by Johnny Tillotson. Tillotson had the most successful recording of the song. The son "Love Potion No. 9" is referenced in this song.

"Poetry in Motion" was also recorded by Bobby Vee on 1961 album Bobby Vee.

In the US Billboard Hot 100, "Poetry in Motion" peaked number 2 in November 1960, kept out of the number 1 Georgia on My Mind by Ray Charles.

Johnny Tillotson is an American singer-songwriter. He enjoyed his greatest success in the early 1960s, when h scored nine top-ten hits on the pop, country, and adult contemporary Billboard charts, including "Poetry in Motion" and the self-penned "It Keeps Right On a-Hurt

Elvis Presley

"Are You Lonesome Tonight?"

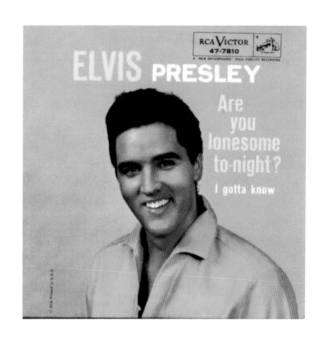

Are You Lonesome Tonight?" In April 1960, after Elvis Presley's two-year service in the United States Army, he recorded the song at the suggestion of manager Colonel Tom Parker; "Are You Lonesome Tonight?" was Parker's wife, Marie Mott's, favourite song. Its release was delayed by RCA Victor executives, who thought the song did not fit Presley's new style. When "Are You Lonesome Tonight?" was released in November 1960 it was an immediate success in the U.S., topping Billboard's Pop Singles chart and reaching number three on the R&B chart.

A month after the song's release, it topped the UK Singles Chart. Presley's version was certified by the Recording Industry Association of America for a Gold Record Award for 1,000,000 copies sold in the United States in 1983.

Petula Clark

"Sailor"

"Sailor" Petula Clark recorded "Sailor" with her regular producer Alan A.Clark, based in Paris since 1957, the song had been pitched "Sailor" by Hatch and orchestra leader Peter Knight while in London for a conference. Originally scheduled for the 20th January 1961, the release of Clark's version of "Sailor" was moved up a week to the 13th January due to Anne Shelton's version of the song being released within the first two weeks of the year. Clark's version of "Sailor" debuted at #18 on the UK Top 50 dated 28th January 1961, becoming Clark's first UK chart entry since "Baby Lover", #12 in March 1958, an intermittent ten UK single releases having failed to chart. A sales total of 250,000 units for Clark's "Sailor" was announced by Pye Records the week of the 18th February 1961 when the single was in its second week at #2: on the chart for the following week: that of 23rd February 1961, Clark's "Sailor" moved to the #1 position of the UK chart.

Everly Brothers

"Walk Right Back"

"Walk Right Back" is a 1961 song by Sonny Curtis that was recorded by The Everly Brothers, and went to No. 7 on the U.S. Billboard Hot 100 chart. Overseas, the song went No. 1 on the UK Singles Chart for three weeks. Originally it was the B-side, and then it was changed to the A-side.

The single, a double A-side in the UK, reached No.1 in the UK Singles Chart on 2 March 1961 for 3 weeks and was the ninth best-selling single of the calendar year 1961 in the U.K. "Ebony Eyes" was initially banned by the B.B.C. from airplay in the U.K. as its lyrics were considered too upsetting to play on the radio.

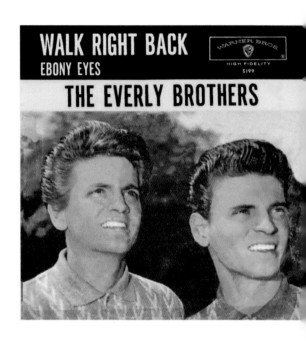

Elvis Presley

"Wooden Heart"

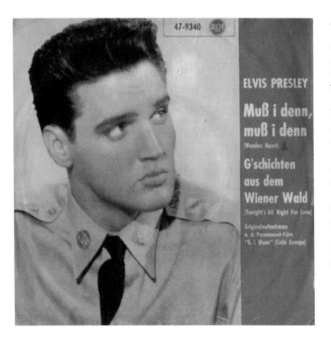

"Wooden Heart" ("Muss i denn" lit. Must I then) is a song recorded by Elvis Presley and featured in the 1960 Elvis Presley film G.I. Blues. The song was a hit single for Presley the UK Singles Chart, reaching No. 1 for six weeks in March and April 1961. The song was released as a single in the United States in November 1964, where it was the B-side to "Blue Christmas". Presley performed the song live during h Dinner Show concert at the Hilton Hotel in Las Vegas in 19 a recording available on the Elvis Presley live album Dinner At Eight. "Wooden Heart" features several lines from the original folk song, written in the German Swabian dialect, a spoken in Württemberg. Marlene Dietrich recorded a versi of the song sometime before 1958, pre-dating Presley, in t original German language, which appears as a B-side on a 1959 version of her single "Lili Marlene".

The Marcels

"Blue Moon"

Blue Moon" In 1961, the Marcels released a new version of the ballad "Blue Moon" that began with the bass singer singing, "bomp-baba-bomp-ba-bomp-ba-bomp-bomp... danga-dang-dang-vadinga-dong-ding...". The record sold over one million copies and was awarded a gold disc. It is featured in the Rock and Roll Hall of Fame's 500 Songs that Shaped Rock and Roll.

The disc went to number one in the U.S. Billboard Hot 100 and UK Singles Chart. In the US, additional revivals in the same vein as "Blue Moon"—"Heartaches" and "My Melancholy Baby"—were less successful, although "Heartaches" peaked at #7 on the Billboard Hot 100 and eventually sold over one million copies worldwide.

Floyd Cramer

"On the Rebound"

"On the Rebound" is a 1961 instrumental by pianist Floyd Cramer. In contrast to most of Cramer's work, which consisted mostly of countrypolitan ballads, "On the Rebound" was an up-tempo rock and roll instrumental. It made No. 4 in the US and No. 1 in the UK.

"On the Rebound" was later featured during the opening credits of the 2009 Oscar-nominated film An Education, which was set in England in 1961.

The Temperance Seven

"You're Driving Me Crazy"

"You're Driving Me Crazy" A cover version by The Temperance Seven, described as an art school band "who were retro before most of pop was even original," was recorded in 1961, reaching number 1 on the UK Singles Chart that May. Their version is a pastiche on the original, and on 1920s dance band music in general, with Paul McDowell's insincere "whispering" helping to highlight this. Music critic Tom Ewing, writing for Freaky Trigger, concurrently described it as "one of the strangest number ones," "one of the most prescient " and "the first meta-pop hit", citing the song's "deliberate, tongue-in-cheek commentary on pop via pop, the world of the dance orchestras pushed flippantly into the TV age," feeling this anticipated Roxy Music and Richard X, but also feeling as many people would have bought the single based on nostalgia as those who bought it due to its cleverness.

Elvis Presley

"Surrender"

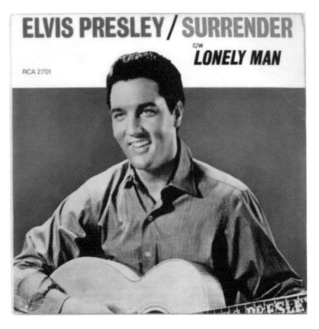

"Surrender" is a #1 song recorded by Elvis Presley and published by Elvis Presley Music in 1961. It is an adaptation by Doc Pomus and Mort Shuman of the music of a 1902 Neapolitan ballad by Giambattista and Ernesto de Curtis entitled "Torna a Surriento" ("Come Back to Sorrento"). It h number one in the US and UK in 1961 and eventually becam one of the best-selling singles of all time. This was one of 25 songs Doc Pomus and Mort Shuman wrote for Elvis Presley.

It has been recorded by many other artists, including Micha Bublé, The Residents, and Il Volo.

Del Shannon

"Runaway"

unaway" was released in February 1961 and was mediately successful. On the 10th April of that year, Del annon appeared on Dick Clark's American Bandstand, lping to catapult it to the number one spot on the Billboard t 100, where it remained for four weeks. Two months later, eached number one on the UK's Record Retailer chart, ending three weeks in that position.

l Shannon re-recorded it in 1967. This version was issued as ingle, and reached No. 122 on Billboard's Bubbling Under e Hot 100. Appearing on Late Night With David Letterman on e 10th February, 1987, Shannon reprised his hit backed by ul Shaffer and the World's Most Dangerous Band. Letterman roduced Shannon as having sold as many as 80,000 singles "Runaway" per day at its height.

The Everly Brothers

"Temptation"

"Temptation" is a popular song published in 1933, with music written by Nacio Herb Brown and lyrics by Arthur Freed.

The song was introduced by Bing Crosby in the 1933 film Going Hollywood. Crosby recorded the song with Lennie Hayton's orchestra on the 22nd October 1933 and it reached the No. 3 spot in the charts of the day during a 12-week stay. He recorded it again with John Scott Trotter's Orchestra on March 3, 1945 and also for his 1954 album Bing: A Musical Autobiography.

The Everly Brothers' version (b/w "Stick With Me Baby", Warner Bros. Records WB5220), released in May 1961, reached #1 in the UK charts. This version also peaked at #27 on the Billboard Hot 100.

Eden Kane

"Well I Ask You"

"Well I Ask You" Recorded in 1961, by Richard Graham Sarstedt, under stage name Eden Kane, as the follow-up to his debut single, "Hot Chocolate Crazy" (1960), "Well I Ask You" was also issued as a single in the UK and reached number one in the UK Singles Chart in August 1961 for one week. It was written by Les Vandyke, arranged by John Keating, and produced by Bunny Lewis, it spent one week at the UK chart pinnacle.

The B-side of the record, released by Decca was "Before I Lose My Mind", also penned by Vandyke.

Helen Shapiro

"You Don't Know"

"You Don't Know" is a 1961 single by Helen Shapiro. It was written by John Schroeder and Mike Hawker and released the Columbia (EMI) label in the United Kingdom on the 29[t] June 1961. "You Don't Know" topped the UK Singles Chart three weeks beginning on the 10th August. The single sold a million copies and earned Shapiro a gold disc.

In Japan, where Shapiro's version also became popular in the song was covered in Japanese by Mieko Hirota, who ha also covered Shapiro's earlier hit "Don't Treat Me Like a Ch

John Leyton

"Johnny Remember Me"

ohnny Remember Me" is a song which became a 1961 UK
ngles Chart #1 hit single for John Leyton, backed by The
Itlaws. It was producer Joe Meek's first #1 production.
counting the haunting – real or imagined – of a young man
 his dead lover, the song is one of the most noted of the
ath ditties' that populated the pop charts, on both sides
 the Atlantic, in the early to mid-1960s. It is distinguished in
rticular by its eerie, echoing sound (a hallmark of Meek's
oduction style) and by the ghostly, foreboding female wails
at form its backing vocal, by Lissa Gray. The recording was
anged by Charles Blackwell. Despite the line, "the girl I
ed who died a year ago" being changed to the more vague
e girl I loved and lost a year ago", the song was banned by
 BBC, along with many other 'death discs', which were
ular at the time.

Shirley Bassey

"Reach for the Stars"

"Reach for the Stars" is a song made popular by Shirley Bassey,
and written by Austrian pop singer/songwriter Udo Jürgens
(with English lyrics by Norman Newell). As a double A-side single
(b/w "Climb Ev'ry Mountain") it went to No. 1 in the UK Singles
Chart for one week in September 1961.

Dame Shirley Veronica Bassey, DBE is a Welsh singer whose
career began in the mid-1950s, and is well known both for her
powerful voice and for recording the theme songs to the James
Bond films Goldfinger (1964), Diamonds Are Forever (1971), and
Moonraker (1979). In January 1959, Bassey became the first
Welsh person to gain a No. 1 single.

In the early and mid-1960s, Bassey had numerous hits in the UK,
and five albums in the Top 15.

The Shadows

"Kon-Tiki"

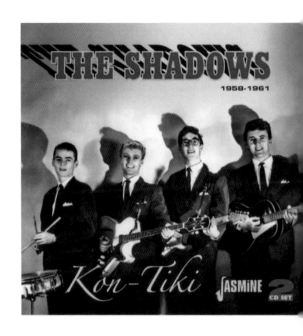

"Kon-Tiki" is an instrumental tune by the Shadows. It became a No. 1 hit in the UK Singles Chart in October 1961. It was the fifth Shadows hit and their second to reach the top of the UK chart. The Shadows (originally known as the Drifters) were an English instrumental rock group. They were Cliff Richard's backing band from 1958 to 1968 and on numerous reunion tours. The Shadows have placed 69 UK charted singles from the 1950s to the 2000s, 35 credited to the Shadows and 34 to Cliff Richard and the Shadows. The group, who were in the forefront of the UK beat-group boom, were the first backing band to emerge as stars. As pioneers of the four-member instrumental format, the band consisted of lead guitar, rhythm guitar, bass guitar and drums. Their range covers pop, rock, surf rock and ballads with a jazz influence.

The Highwaymen

"Michael"

"Michael, Row the Boat Ashore "is an African-American spiritual first noted during the American Civil War at St. He Island, one of the Sea Islands of South Carolina. The best known recording was released in 1960 by the U.S. folk ban The Highwaymen; that version briefly reached number-one status as a single.

It was sung by former slaves whose owners had abandone the island before the Union navy arrived to enforce a block Charles Pickard Ware was an abolitionist and Harvard grad who had come to supervise the plantations on St. Helena Island from 1862 to 1865, and he wrote down the song in music notation as he heard the freedmen sing it. Ware's co William Francis Allen reported in 1863 that the former sla sang the song as they rowed him in a boat across Station Creek.

Helen Shapiro

"Walkin' Back to Happiness"

"Walkin' Back to Happiness" is a 1961 single by Helen Shapiro. The song was written by John Schroeder and Mike Hawker. With backing orchestrations by Norrie Paramor, the song was released in the United Kingdom on the Columbia (EMI) label on the 29th September 1961. It was number one in the UK for three weeks beginning 19th October, but only reached #100 on the US Billboard Hot 100, Shapiro's only US chart appearance. The single sold over a million copies and earned Helen Shapiro a golden disc.

Helen Kate Shapiro is a British pop singer, jazz singer, and actress. She is best known for her two 1961 UK chart toppers, "You Don't Know" and "Walkin' Back to Happiness", both recorded when she was just fourteen years old.

Elvis Presley

"Little Sister"

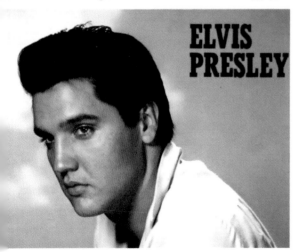

LITTLE SISTER

Are you lonesome to-night
His latest flame - I gotta know

86.304
MEDIUM

"Little Sister" is a rock and roll song written by Doc Pomus and Mort Shuman. It was originally released as a single in 1961 by American singer Elvis Presley, who enjoyed a No. 5 hit with it on the Billboard Hot 100. The single (as a double A-side with "(Marie's the Name) His Latest Flame") also reached No. 1 in the UK Singles Chart. Lead guitar was played by Hank Garland, with backing vocals by the Jordanaires featuring the distinctive bass voice of Ray Walker.

Elvis Presley performs the song as part of a medley with "Get Back" in the 1970 rockumentary film Elvis: That's the Way It Is. The song would later be covered by such artists as Dwight Yoakam, Robert Plant, The Nighthawks, The Staggers, Pearl Jam, and Ry Cooder. Cooder's version was a number-one hit in New Zealand.

Frankie Vaughan

"Tower of Strength"

"Tower of Strength" is a song written by Burt Bacharach and Bob Hilliard. Frankie Vaughan CBE was an English singer of easy listening and traditional pop music, who recorded more than 80 singles in his lifetime. He was known as "Mr. Moonlight" after one of his early hits.

Frankie Vaughan released this version as a single that peaked at No. 1 on the UK Singles Chart in 1961. He recorded a large number of songs that were covers of United States hit songs, including Perry Como's "Kewpie Doll," Jimmie Rodgers' "Kisses Sweeter than Wine," Boyd Bennett's "Seventeen" (also covered in the US by the Fontane Sisters), Jim Lowe's "The Green Door," and (with the Kaye Sisters), the Fleetwood's' "Come Softly to Me". In 1956, his cover of "The Green Door" reached No. 2 in the UK Singles Chart.

Danny Williams

"Moon River"

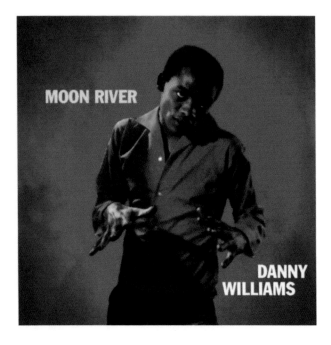

"Moon River". Danny Williams was a South African-born British pop singer who earned the nickname "Britain's John Mathis", for his smooth and stylish way with a ballad. He is best known for his 1961 UK number one version of "Moon River" and his 1964 U.S. top ten hit, "White on White".

Born in Port Elizabeth, Eastern Cape, South Africa, Danny Williams won a talent contest at the age of 14 and joined a touring show called Golden City Dixies that played through South Africa. In 1959, the show came to London where Williams impressed EMI's Norman Newell, who signed the young singer to a recording contract. He was to spend most his life in the United Kingdom, where at first he made a few moderately successful singles, mainly popular ballads, before scoring a number one hit with his cover version of "Moon River" in 1961.

WORLD EVENTS 1961

1st Australia became the second nation to permit the sale of the birth control pill, and the first to allow the Scherer oral contraceptive, with brand name of Anovlar. The G.D. Searle pill Enovid had been permitted in the United States in May 1960.

3rd In the worst airplane crash in the history of Finland, all 25 persons on Aero OY Flight 311 were killed when the DC-3 crashed shortly after take-off from Vaasa while en route to Kronoby. The plane impacted in trees six miles away, near the village of Koivulahti. A subsequent investigation concluded that both the pilot and co-pilot had been drinking as recently as five hours before take-off.

th John F. Kennedy was formally elected as the 35th President of the United States, as a joint session of the U.S. Congress witnessed the counting of the electoral vote. U.S. Vice-President Richard Nixon, who had opposed Kennedy in the 1960 election, formally announced the result, saying, "I now declare John F. Kennedy elected president." The results were 303 votes for Kennedy, 219 for Nixon, and 15 for U.S. Senator Harry F. Byrd, Jr.

th In the final week of his administration, U.S. President Dwight D. Eisenhower issued an Executive Order that closed a loophole that allowed American people and companies to own gold outside of the United States. Since 1933, persons and companies under American jurisdiction were barred from buying, selling or owning gold within the U.S., but were not prohibited from hoarding it outside of the country. The new order directed that all Americans who held gold coins, gold bars, and foreign gold securities and gold certificates, would have to dispose of their holdings no later than the 1st June. The move came after the U.S. trade deficit had grown by ten billion dollars over the previous three years.

th In New Zealand, the filling of Lake Ohakuri began. Within two weeks, a reservoir of nearly five square miles was created and a supply of hydroelectric power was created. At the same time, two of the world's largest geysers—the 295-foot-high Minquini and the 180-foot-high Orakeikorako—were covered over and made extinct.

st Loaded with 16 nuclear tipped Polaris A-1 missiles, the submarine USS George Washington completed its first "deterrent patrol", after having remained submerged for a record 66 consecutive days.

January

24th | A B-52 Stratofortress, with two Mark 39 hydrogen bombs, crashed on a farm at the community of Faro, miles (19 km) north of near Goldsboro, North Carolina. Three USAF officers were killed. One of the bom went partially through its arming sequence, as five of its six safety switches failed. The one remaining switch prevented a 24 megaton nuclear explosion.

25th | One Hundred and One Dalmatians, the 17th full-length animated film by Walt Disney, had its world premiere, at 8:00 pm the Florida Theatre in St. Petersburg, Florida.

29th | Five days after arriving in New York after hitchhiking from Madison, Wisconsin, 21-year-old musician B Dylan met his idol Woody Guthrie. After hearing Dylan sing, Guthrie is said to have remarked "He's a talented boy. Gonna go far." Dylan settled in Greenwich Village and found fame in the protest folk mus

30th | Disenchanted with life in the Soviet Union, American defector Lee Harvey Oswald wrote to President Kennedy's newly appointed U.S. Secretary of the Navy, John Connally, to ask for a reversal of Oswald's dishonourable discharge from the United States Marines. The letter was never acted upon, and on November 22, 1963, Oswald would shoot both Kennedy and Connally.

31st | Ham the Chimp, a 37-pound (17 kg) male, was rocketed into space aboard Mercury-Redstone 2, in a te the Project Mercury capsule. His successful 16½-minute flight demonstrated to American NASA offici that the capsule could safely carry human astronauts into space.

February

1st | The push-button telephone was put into public service for the first time, as Bell Telephone test market its "Touch-Tone" service for its customers in the cities of Carnegie, Pennsylvania and Findlay, Ohio.

3rd | Operation Looking Glass began, as the first of a series of Boeing EC-135 jets went into the air on order the Strategic Air Command. For more than 30 years, an EC-135 was always in the air, with the capabilit taking direct control of the United States' bombers and missiles in the event of the destruction of the S command post near Omaha. As one jet "Doomsday Plane" was preparing to land, another was already aloft. The program continued, with E4A jets later replacing the EC-135s, until the fall of the Soviet Unic

4th | Sputnik 7 was launched by the Soviet Union and placed into Earth orbit. Although reported as a succes that it was the heaviest object (14,300 pounds) into orbit at that time.

th Movie actress Marilyn Monroe voluntarily checked herself into the Cornell University Medical Center (under the pseudonym "Faye Miller") after being driven there by her psychiatrist, Dr. Marianne Kris. Admitted on the premise that she would be treated for exhaustion, Monroe was instead taken to the Payne Whitney Psychiatric Clinic and found "the worst fear of her life come true", being locked inside a padded cell. After three days, she was permitted to make a phone call and reached her ex-husband, baseball star Joe DiMaggio, who flew to New York City and affected her release.

th Three Vautour fighter jets of the French Air Force attacked an Il-18 plane that was carrying Leonid Brezhnev, who at the time was the ceremonial head of state of the Soviet Union and was on his way to the Republic of Guinea for a state visit. When Brezhnev's plane strayed into the airspace of French Algeria, it was intercepted by the three fighters, one of which fired bursts of tracer bullets and forced Brezhnev's plane to make an emergency landing in Morocco. The French Foreign Ministry apologized the next day.

th A total solar eclipse was visible in parts of the Northern Hemisphere from France to the Soviet Union, with the Black Sea port of Rostov-on-Don being the midpoint of the greatest eclipse.

rd Duncan Carse was dropped off alone at the British Antarctic island of South Georgia, for an eighteen-month attempt to become a latter-day Robinson Crusoe. HMS Owen brought him to the uninhabited south side of the island with 12 tons of supplies and a prefabricated hut, at Ducloz Head. The hut and much of the supplies would be swept away by a wave on the 20th May, forcing Carse to survive on what he had been able to save. He would finally be able to signal a ship, the Petrel, on the 13th September.

th Paul Bikle set a record for altitude for a sailplane, reaching 46,266 feet (14,102 meters) after catching a Sierra Wave in the skies near California's Mount Whitney. The record would remain unbroken more than 50 years later.

rch

nd At the age of 79, artist Pablo Picasso married 35-year-old Jacqueline Roque. The two remained together until his death in 1973.

th At a press conference at Andrews Air Force Base, spokesmen for the U.S. Air Force Research and Development command announced that they had developed an atomic clock "so accurate that its biggest error would not exceed one second in 1271 years", and, at 62 pounds, light enough that it could be used on aircraft in place of the existing system of crystal oscillators. Conventional atomic clock units, though more accurate, weighed over 600 pounds and were impractical for flight.

^h Max Conrad, "the Flying Grandfather", circumnavigated the Earth in 8 days, 18 hours and 49 minutes, setting a new world record for a light airplane, breaking the previous mark, set in 1959, of 25 days.

^h The first definite proof that a signal could be sent to Venus and returned to Earth, using radar astronomy, was made by the Jet Propulsion Laboratory. Transmission was sent from the Goldstone Tracking Station in California at a 2,388 megacycle frequency, traveling 35 million miles to Venus and then back to Earth, in a little more than six minutes. Signals had been bounced off of Venus before, but never received back clearly enough to be "immediately detectable".

14th | The first phase of the creation of the New English Bible, begun in 1946 by the Joint Committee on the N Translation of the Bible", was completed with the publication of the revised New Testament. Relying or re-examination of the oldest texts and conveyance of original meanings into modern English, the "new Testament" was released to coincide with the 350th anniversary of the March 1611 publication of the K James Version of the Bible.

16th | The 18th Golden Globe Awards were held. Winners included Burt Lancaster (Best Actor – Drama), Gree Garson (Best Actress – Drama) and Spartacus (Best Film – Drama).

21st | The Beatles— John, Paul, George and Stu (Stuart Sutcliffe) — began the first of nearly 300 regular performances at The Cavern Club in Liverpool. Sutcliffe left the band three months later. Continuing wit Ringo Starr, the group's final appearance at the Cavern Club was on the 3rd August 1963.

24th | A Mercury-Redstone BD rocket was launched from Cape Canaveral, Florida, on one final test flight to certify its safety for human transport. As with earlier Soviet tests, the American space capsule carried a test dummy. The spacecraft reached an altitude of 115 miles and was recovered in the Atlantic 8 minut after launch. Stopped by Wernher von Braun from going, Alan Shepard had volunteered to take the flig and would have become the first man to travel into outer space. Less than three weeks later, Soviet cosmonaut Yuri Gagarin would, on the 12th April, would reach the milestone. Shepard would reach spac though not orbit, on the 5th May.

28th | U.S. President John F. Kennedy informed Congress that, as part of the proposed $43.8 billion defence budget, he was cancelling the Pye Wacket project, an experimental lenticular-form air-to-air missile, ar the B-70 nuclear-powered airplane. Kennedy declared that "As a power which will never strike first, ou hopes for anything close to an absolute deterrent must rest on weapons which come from hidden, moving, or invulnerable bases which will not be wiped out by a surprise attack," and lobbied instead fo ten additional Polaris nuclear submarines and an increased Minuteman nuclear arsenal.

XB-70 Valkyrie

Cockpit of XB-70 Valkyrie

30th | Actor Ronald Reagan gave a speech entitled 'Encroaching Control' to the Phoenix Chamber of Commer This speech was considered by some historians to be his finest and the moment his political career tru began.

1st With the approval of the Food and Drug Directorate, the morning sickness suppressant thalidomide went on sale for the first time in Canada, marketed by Richardson-Merrill under the name Kevadon. The Horner Company would begin sales of its own version, Talimol, in October. Despite evidence later in the year that the drug caused birth defects, sales were not halted in Canada until the 21st March 1962, after four million tablets had sold to expectant mothers.

5th Singer Barbra Streisand made her national television debut, as a guest on Tonight Starring Jack Paar. In TV listings, both of her names were misspelled, as "Barbara Strysand".

8th Shortly after 4:00 am, the British passenger ship MV Dara exploded off Dubai. In the fire and in panic during the rescue, 238 passengers and crew died, while another 565 were rescued. The ship sank two days later while being towed. A British Admiralty court concluded a year later that an anti-tank mine, "deliberately placed by a person or persons unknown", had "almost certainly" caused the explosion.

9th The last of the streetcars of Los Angeles was retired, after 136 passengers boarded the last scheduled Pacific Electric Railway red car to ride the 18 mile rail line to Long Beach. A charter car departed 10 minutes later. The network had been formed in 1902, but the interurban tracks were gradually removed after World War II.

Gary Player of South Africa became the first foreigner to win the American Masters Tournament, taking the event by one stroke. On the very last hole, the leader, Arnold Palmer had to take six strokes.

The preliminary stage of the Bay of Pigs Invasion commenced as eight Douglas B-26B Invader bombers attacked Cuban airfields at San Antonio de Los Baños, Ciudad Libertad, and Santiago de Cuba airport. The B-26s had been prepared by the CIA on behalf of Brigade 2506, and painted in false flag markings of the Cuban air force. They had flown from Nicaragua with crews of Cuban exiles, and the purpose of Operation Puma was to destroy armed aircraft of the Cuban air force in advance of the main invasion. Shortly after the attacks, another B-26 flew to Miami with false battle damage, and the pilot falsely claimed to be one of several Cuban defectors. At the United Nations, the Cuban Foreign Minister accused the US of aggressive air attacks against Cuba. The U.S. ambassador to the UN Adlai Stevenson stated that US armed forces would not "under any conditions" intervene in Cuba. He was later embarrassed to realize that the CIA had lied to him and to Secretary of State Dean Rusk.

April

17th Thousands of troops began the Bay of Pigs Invasion of Cuba at 1:00 in the morning local time, as Operat[ion] Zapata got under way. The first group of a force of about 1,300 Cuban exiles of Brigade 2506 made an amphibious landing at Playa Girón, a beach at the Bahia de Cochinos ("Bay of Pigs" in Spanish) on the southern coast of Cuba. They had been trained by the CIA in Guatemala, and then embarked in Nicarag[ua] on four freighter ships chartered by the CIA, and escorted to Cuban waters by a large U.S. Navy task for[ce]. A second group of attackers landed 35 km further northwest in the bay at Playa Larga. By about 06:30, [the] freighter ships and landing craft still unloading troops, vehicles and equipment were attacked by Sea Fu[ry] fighter-bombers and T-33 jets of the Cuban air force. At about 07:30, 177 invading paratroopers were dropped at four locations north of the landing areas. By about 09:00, one of the freighters had been damaged and beached, and another was then sunk in the bay by air-to-ground rockets. The surviving vessels withdrew south to international waters. By the end of the day, four attacking B-26 bombers had been shot down by T-33s and ground fire, and invading troops had come under fire from Cuban militia regular troops.

19th Air attacks were made by B-26s against advancing Cuban ground forces. Combat air patrols, with strict rules of engagement, were flown by unmarked US Navy A4D Skyhawk jets from USS Essex, but they fail[ed] to prevent two bombers being shot down by Cuban aircraft, killing four Americans of the Alabama National Guard employed by the CIA as aircrew trainers. By dusk, about 17:30, Brigade 2506 ground for[ces] had retreated to the beaches, then surrendered or dispersed into neighbouring swamps. About 114 Brigade ground troops, and 176 Cuban ground forces, were killed in combat. With the failure of the Ba[y of] Pigs Invasion, Cuba would take 1,189 of the invaders as prisoners of war and try them for treason. On December 24, 1962, the last group of 1,113 prisoners would be released in exchange for $53,000,000 worth of food and medicine.

23rd Judy Garland performed a legendary comeback concert at Carnegie Hall in New York City, receiving a standing ovation as she arrived on stage, and five minutes of cheering. Variety critic Gordon Cox Tom Moon, 1,000 Recordings to Hear Before You Die: A Listener's Life List (Workman Publishing, 2008) described the event as "the greatest night in show business history". The live performance was recorde[d] as a Grammy award-winning and bestselling album, Judy at Carnegie Hall.

27th At 10 seconds after midnight in Freetown, the green white and blue flag of the Dominion of Sierra Leor[e] replaced Britain's Union Jack as the former British colony for freed slaves became an independent nation.[68] A British anti-slavery society had purchased West African land in 1787 from King Waimban[a] and Britain created the colony in 1808. Later in the day, Sir Milton Margai took office as the nation's fir[st] Prime Minister, and accepted the new constitution from Prince Edward, Duke of Kent, who was appea[ring] on behalf of his cousin, Queen Elizabeth II. The former colonial governor, Sir Maurice Dorman, became [the] first Governor-General. Opposition leader Siaka Stevens, who would become President when the Dominion became a Republic in 1971, was kept under house arrest until ceremonies were over.

29th Westward Television became the exclusive holder of the independent television franchise for the Sout[h] West of England, and would retain it for twenty years.

30th The first nuclear-powered Soviet submarine, K-19, was commissioned.

st For the first time since Fidel Castro took power, an American airplane was hijacked to Cuba. A man who was listed on the manifest as "Cofresi Elpirata", after the 19th century Caribbean pirate Roberto Cofresí, entered the cockpit of a National Airlines flight that was en route from Miami to Key West, then forced the pilot to fly to Havana. Castro allowed the plane, its crew and all but one of its passengers, to return to the U.S. the next day. Staying behind was "Cofresi", Miami electrician Antuilio Ortiz, who would live comfortably in Cuba for two years before becoming homesick for the U.S. After being incarcerated several times in Cuban prisons, Ortiz would finally be allowed to leave in 1975, and would spend four years in an American prison for the 1961 crime.

th Commander Malcolm Ross and Lieutenant Commander Victor A. Prather set a new record for the highest balloon flight while testing full pressure flight suits. The two U.S. Navy officers ascended to 113,740 feet (34.67 km) over the Gulf of Mexico before landing successfully. Commander Ross was successfully transported to USS Antietam (CVS-36) by helicopter. Lt. Comm. Prather subsequently slipped from the sling and drowned after his suit flooded.

th Carry Back, ridden by Johnny Sellers, won the Kentucky Derby. The racehorse, bred from a mare that had cost only $300, would earn more than a million dollars for his owners. Carry Back won the Preakness Stakes, but failed to win the third part of U.S. horse racing's Triple Crown, finishing 7th in the Belmont Stakes.

th A brush fire in Hollywood, California, destroyed 24 houses, including the home of author Aldous Huxley, who lost almost all of his unpublished manuscripts and works in progress.

th The first fatality in the history of Little League Baseball occurred during an evening game in Temple City, California. Nine-year-old Barry Babcock was struck in the chest by a pitched ball, with impact above his heart, and collapsed and died from a cardiac dysrhythmia. One week later, the second fatality in Little League baseball took place when ten-year-old George McCormick, of Park Ridge, Illinois, was struck in the head by a batted ball during practice.

th American athlete Ralph Boston broke the long jump world record at Modesto, California, with a distance of 8.24 metres (27 feet, 4 inches).

th Peter Benenson's article "The Forgotten Prisoners" was published in several internationally read newspapers, and inspired the founding of the human rights organization Amnesty International.

th A West Virginia couple, Mr. and Mrs. Alderson Muncy of Paynesville, West Virginia, became the first American food stamp recipients under a pilot program of the U.S. Department of Agriculture, being tested in eight communities. For the month of June, the Muncys received $95 worth of food coupons for their household of fifteen people, and made the first purchase at Henderson's Supermarket.

th KLM Flight 897 crashed at 1:19 in the morning, shortly after taking off from Lisbon, ultimately bound for Caracas. High winds and driving rains brought the DC-8 jet down into the ocean off of the coast of Portugal, with wreckage and bodies washing onto the beach. All 61 persons on board were killed.

t Presidents John F. Kennedy of the United States and Charles De Gaulle of France met in Paris. Making her first trip to Europe as First Lady, Jackie Kennedy charmed the crowds as she arrived for dinner at the Elysee Palace. Her new hairstyle, created by the Paris coiffeur Alexandre made fashion news worldwide.

June

1st | The birth control pill was introduced in West Germany, as Anovlar, developed by the Berlin pharmaceu... company Schering AG, became available for prescription.

3rd | Died: "G. I. Joe", 18, British war pigeon who was credited with saving the lives of 1,000 soldiers of the British 56th Infantry. On October 18, 1943, the division had taken control of the village of Calvi Vecchia Italy, shortly before the RAF was preparing to make an air strike there. The pigeon flew 20 miles to the airfield just as seven RAF bombers were preparing to depart, and the mission was aborted in time.

7th | The Sony Corporation made its first public stock offering in the United States, with two million shares offered at $1.75 a share on Wall Street. Within two hours, all shares had been sold.

8th | The first public demonstration of a jet pack was made by Bell Laboratories test pilot Harold Graham, wh... flew the Bell Rocket Belt at Fort Eustis, Virginia before a crowd of several hundred military officers and their guests.

14th | A custom-built 1961 Lincoln Continental convertible was delivered to the White House for use of Presid... Kennedy. Kennedy would be assassinated in the car on the 22nd November 1963.

18th | The Belgian Grand Prix was won by Phil Hill, who finished 0.7 seconds ahead of Wolfgang von Trips. Firs... second and third place were taken by Ferraris.

23rd | USAF Major Robert M. White became the first person to fly an airplane faster than one mile per secon... (3,600 miles per hour) and the first to pass Mach 5. White was piloting an X-15 over California after tak... off from Edwards Air Force Base, and attained a maximum speed of 3,690 mph. White, who on the 7th March had been first to reach Mach 4 first person to travel faster than Mach 4, would become the first... reach Mach 6, on the 9th November.

26th | Ernest Hemingway was released from hospitalization for the last time, after spending two months at th... psychiatric hospital at the Mayo Clinic for suicidal behaviour. The renowned author would shoot himse... six days later.

30th | In a pivotal event in the history of professional wrestling, a record crowd of 38,622 fans turned out to Chicago's Comiskey Park. Buddy Rogers defeated reigning National Wrestling Alliance champion Pat O'Connor for the NWA World Heavyweight Championship.

In a meeting at the Kremlin, Soviet leader Nikita Khrushchev warned Sir Frank Roberts, the British Ambassador, that Britain and France should avoid joining the United States in going to war over West Berlin, telling him "Six hydrogen bombs would be quite enough to annihilate the British Isles, and nine would take care of France."

At 4:15 am, the Soviet submarine K-19 developed a leak in its nuclear reactor, while conducting exercises in the North Atlantic near the Norwegian island of Jan Mayen. The rupture of the primary coolant system caused the water pressure in the aft reactor to drop to zero and causing failure of the coolant pumps. Eight crew members died within three weeks of the accident, and others were successfully treated for deadly doses of radiation.

Following a contest to come up with a name for an artificial lake, near Mount Isa, Queensland, Australia, created in 1958 by a dam on the Leichhardt River, the winning entry was selected from 471 suggested names. Lake Moondarra, the entry suggested by 9 year old Danny Driscoll, is said to have been an Australian aboriginal (Murri language) name that means, "plenty of rain, also thunder".

Eight people were killed when lightning struck a tobacco curing barn in Clinton, North Carolina, where they had taken shelter from a storm. Although they were inside, the victims had been sitting on metal surfaces when the bolt hit.

The Singleton Bank rail crash occurred in Lancashire, England, when the 8:50 diesel multiple unit passenger train from Colne} to Fleetwood collided with the rear of a ballast train at about 45 miles per hour (72 km/h). Seven people, including the driver, were killed, and another 116 were injured.

The first regularly scheduled in-flight movie service began, as a TWA flight from New York to Los Angeles showed By Love Possessed to its first class customers.

After two years of living and working in Minsk, American defector Lee Harvey Oswald applied to the Soviet Union for an exit visa so that he could return to the United States. He, his wife and daughter were finally granted permission to leave on the 30th May 1962.

The first wristwatch made in India, manufactured by Hindustan Machine Tools (HMT), was presented to Prime Minister Jawaharlal Nehru in Bangalore. The company had been set up in collaboration with the Japanese manufacturer Citizen Holdings, maker of the Citizen watch.

Using an IBM 7090 computer, researchers Daniel Shanks and John W. Wrench, Jr., were able to calculate the value of pi to 100,000 digits for the first time. In 1949, prior to the use of computers, the first 1,120 digits had been found "by hand" using a desk calculator. The same year, the ENIAC computer took 70 hours to reach 2,037 decimal places. The 10,000 mark had been broken in 1957 on an IBM 704 in 100 minutes. The IBM 7090 operation took 8 hours and 43 minutes.

The first NASCAR race (referred to at the time as the Volunteer 500) at Bristol Motor Speedway, the shortest track on the circuit, was won by Jack Smith (who started the race) and Johnny Allen, who finished after Smith's foot was burned by his car.

Ireland submitted its first ever application to join the then European Economic Community.

August

3rd | The nuclear powered submarine USS Thresher was commissioned at the Portsmouth, New Hampshire Naval Shipyard. On the 10th April 1963, the Thresher would be lost along with all 129 of its crew during deep diving tests.

5th | Berlin Crisis: At the close of the meeting in Moscow, the Warsaw Pact nations announced that they had agreed unanimously to sign a separate peace treaty with East Germany with the objective of ending the occupation of American, British and French troops in Berlin. That day, the number of East Germans flee into West Berlin had reached 1,500 or "one per minute". At the same meeting, Soviet Premier Khrushch gave East German leader Walter Ulbricht his approval for closing the boundaries of East Berlin with a barbed-wire fence.

8th | The Fantastic Four team of superheroes was introduced by Marvel Comics, as issue #1 of the comic boo of the same name, post-dated for November, was placed on American newsstands and stores for the fi time.

13th | Construction of the Berlin Wall, ordered by Walter Ulbricht, began at 2:00 a.m. Central European Time with the erection of a barbed-wire fence along the line between East Berlin and West Berlin, the diggin trenches along streets at the border, and the closure of railroad lines. The corridors from West Berlin t West Germany were not disturbed, and the other three Allied powers did not move troops or protest about the action. (The wall would eventually be demolished on the 9th November 1989)

20th | In order to show American support for West Berlin and reinforce the 11,000 Allied soldiers there, a con of 1,500 U.S. Army troops was sent by President Kennedy on 110-mile (180 km) trip through East Germany, along the autobahn from Helmstedt to Berlin. More than 100 trucks with men, weapons and supplies were accompanied by jeeps and three M-41 tanks. The Soviet Army abided by prior agreemer to permit American, British and French armies to use the Helmstedt-Berlin highway as a corridor, and 1st Battle Group, 18th Infantry Regiment of the 18th U.S. Infantry was greeted in West Berlin by U.S. V President Lyndon Johnson.

23rd | A6 murder case: Michael Gregsten was killed at Deadman's Hill on the A6 highway, near the village of Clophill, Bedfordshire, England. Gregsten's companion, Valerie Storie, was raped, shot and left for dea James Hanratty was later convicted and executed for the murder.

rd The minimum wage in the United States was raised to $1.15 an hour. All covered persons hired on or after that date would still receive the previous minimum of $1.00 an hour. Minimum wage 50 years later would be $7.25 an hour.

th A secured telephone line between the White House in Washington DC, and the Admiralty House in London, was set up in order for the U.S. President and the British Prime Minister to communicate directly, in real time, with their conversations scrambled. President Kennedy and Prime Minister Macmillan used the line for the first time in October.

th France's President Charles de Gaulle escaped an assassination attempt as his limousine took him from Paris to his country home at Colombey-les-Deux-Églises. A bomb with eight pounds of plastique had been placed on the President's route between the cities of Nogent-sur-Seine and Romilly-sur-Seine, and an inflammable mixture exploded in flames as the car passed over. The plastique failed to detonate. There were as many as 30 attempts to kill de Gaulle, of which this attempt and an August 22, 1962, machine gunning of his limousine, came closest to success. After the 1962 attempt, de Gaulle pushed through major constitutional reforms to increase his power.

th While driving a Ferrari during the F1 Italian Grand Prix at Monza, Germany's Wolfgang von Trips, 33, crashed into the infield, killing 18 spectators and him. Eleven bystanders died at the scene, while 7 more of the 26 injured died later. The crash happened on the second lap, when Von Trips was struck from behind by Jimmy Clark's Lotus. The race continued for the next two hours, with the bodies of the dead covered with newspapers, not moved until after the race's end. Prior to the final race of the season, Von Trips had been in the lead for the World Driving Championship. The race win, and the title, went instead to Phil Hill.

th Two weeks after the Soviet Union resumed nuclear testing; the United States carried out Operation Nougat and exploded a nuclear bomb for the first time since the 30th October 1958. While the Soviet tests were atmospheric, the American tests were conducted underground at the Nevada Test Site.

rd At 3:45 am, Antonio Abertondo arrived in Dover and became the first person to swim across the English Channel and right back again, resting for only ten minutes between crossings. Abertondo had departed England on the 20th September at 8:35 am, arriving nearly 19 hours later in Wissant on the coast of France. After his brief break, Abertondo began his swim back to England.

h Department of the Army Message 578636 designated the green beret as the exclusive headgear of the U.S. Army Special Forces, giving the group their nickname of the "Green Berets".

h The first episode of TV prime-time cartoon series Top Cat was aired on the ABC network in the U.S.

h The word "ain't" was accepted into the English language with the publication of the Third Edition of the Merriam-Webster, the first completely new edition since 1944. Merriam President Gordon J. Oallan had announced the controversial decision on the 6th September, noting that "ain't" was one of thousands of new words that had been added.

h Minutes after Fidel Castro announced that he was going to "clean up" Havana, the last casinos in Cuba was closed. At the time of the revolution, there had been 25 gambling casinos. Five were left, all in government operated hotels, at the time of the order.

October

1st | In the UK soap Coronation Street, two major characters, Harry Hewitt and Concepta Riley, married on screen.

7th | 1961 Derby Aviation crash: A Douglas C47 Dakota 4 operated by Derby Aviation, a subsidiary of British Midland Airways, crashed in the Pyrennes Mountains at Mont Canigou in France. All 34 people on board, mostly a group of British tourists who were on holiday to make a tour of Spain, were killed.

8th | The first of at least 134 residents of East Berlin escaped to the West through a manhole that led to an underground sewer that ran underneath the Berlin Wall. West German students Dieter Thieme and Detlef Girmann organized the Unternehmen Reisebüro, also called the "Girmann Group". The operation lasted for four nights until East German police learned what was happening and closed off the route.

11th | Flying an X-15, USAF Major Robert White set a record for highest flight by an airplane, reaching an altitude of 215,000 feet, more than 40 miles above the Earth, 8 miles higher than the previous record. On his descent, the outer windshield of the X-15 cracked, but White was unharmed.

20th | The first launch of an armed nuclear warhead on a submarine-launched ballistic missile took place, when a Soviet Golf-class submarine (Project 629) fired an R-13 (SS N-4 Sark) missile from underwater. The 1.45 megaton warhead detonated on the Novaya Zemlya Test Range in the Arctic Ocean. Although the U.S. had test-fired unarmed Polaris missiles, the first American SLBM nuclear detonation would not take place until the 6th May 1962.

22nd | Berlin Crisis: Two months after construction of the Berlin Wall, E. Allan Lightner, Jr., Deputy Chief of the U.S. Mission in West Berlin, and his wife, were stopped when he tried to drive his car across the border after refusing to produce identification while crossing at Checkpoint Charlie, to attend the opera in East Berlin. General Lucius Clay dispatched troops, backed up by several tanks and military vehicles, to the Checkpoint. The Lightners were escorted into East Berlin by eight U.S. military policemen. Over the next three days, what started as a trivial incident escalated into a confrontation between the U.S. and the Soviet Union.

27th | Berlin Crisis: Five days after the initial incident involving Albert Hemsing, 33 Soviet tanks drove to the Brandenburg Gate to confront American tanks on the other side of the border. Ten of the tanks continued to Friedrichstraße, stopping 50 to 100 metres from the checkpoint on the Soviet side of the sector boundary. The standoff between the tanks of the two nations continued for 16 hours before both sides withdrew.

30th | The Soviet Union detonated a 50-megaton yield hydrogen bomb known as Tsar Bomba over Novaya Zemlya, in the largest man-made explosion ever. Too large to be fit inside even the largest available warplane, the weapon was suspended from a Tupolev Tu-95 piloted by A.E. Durnovtsev, a Hero of the Soviet Union. A parachute slowed the bomb's descent so that the airplane could have time to climb away from the fireball, and at an altitude of four kilometers, was exploded at 8:33 AM GMT. Although the news drew protests around the world, the event was not reported in the Soviet press.

31st | Shortly after 10:00 pm in Moscow, Joseph Stalin's body was removed from the Lenin Mausoleum and reburied outside the Kremlin as part of his successor's policy of de-Stalinization.

rd United Artists announced the selection of actor Sean Connery to portray James Bond in the upcoming film Dr. No. Patrick McGoohan turned down the role, and Roger Moore (who would begin portraying Bond in 1973) was unavailable due to his commitments on the TV show The Saint.

th U.S. Amateur golf champion Jack Nicklaus, a 21-year-old senior at Ohio State University announced at a press conference that he was turning professional. Nicklaus would go on to win 19 major championships, including six Masters tournaments and six PGA Championships.

th An Atlas missile, launched from the United States with a squirrel monkey on board, exploded 30 seconds after lift-off while being tested for a 5,000 mile flight. The body of "Goliath", the 24 ounce passenger, was found in the wreckage two days later.

th Ten days after pressure blew the cap from a natural gas well in the Sahara Desert in Algeria, the "world's biggest fire" started, sending flames 600 feet high. Firefighting expert Red Adair would extinguish the blaze on the 29th April 1962, with 660 pounds of dynamite.

th Rembrandt's Aristotle Contemplating a Bust of Homer sold to the Metropolitan Museum of Art for 2.3 million dollars, becoming the most expensive painting in the world.

Aristotle Contemplating a Bust of Homer   **Rembrandt**

th Michael Rockefeller, son of New York Governor, and later Vice President Nelson Rockefeller, disappeared off of the coast of New Guinea. His body was never found and a court in White Plains, New York, officially declared him dead on the 31st January 1964. The younger Rockefeller left an estate worth $660,000.

d Andy Warhol wrote gallerist Muriel Latow a check for $50, thought to have been payment for coming up with the idea of soup cans as subject matter for his art.

November

26th | West German pharmaceutical manufacturer Grünenthal GmbH became the first company to take thalidomide off of the market, nine days after the first report of its link to birth defects was published. Distillers Company Ltd. removed the drug from British distribution on December 21st.

29th | The United States successfully placed a chimpanzee, Enos, into orbit around the Earth, clearing the way the first American astronaut to break the pull of Earth's gravity. Enos lifted off from Cape Canaveral on board Mercury-Atlas 5 at 9:07 am, made two circuits of the globe, and was recovered safely at 12:28 pr the Atlantic Ocean. After the successful flight, NASA announced that one of two men would become the first to be sent into orbit, settling on John Glenn or Donald "Deke" Slayton.

December

1st | Britannia Airways was a charter airline based in the UK. It was founded in 1961 as Euravia and became world's largest holiday airline. Britannia's main bases were at London Gatwick, London Stansted, Londo Luton, Cardiff, Bristol, East Midlands, Birmingham, Manchester, Newcastle, Leeds Bradford, Edinburgh, and Glasgow and had its headquarters at Britannia House in Luton, Bedfordshire. Britannia was origina charter operator for Universal Sky Tours and later for Thomson holidays where it became the in-house airline with a fleet of Boeing jet aircraft. In 2000, Thomson Travel Group, and thereby Britannia Airway were acquired by Preussag AG (TUI Group) of Germany. As part of a wider reorganisation of TUI's UK operations in September 2004, Britannia was rebranded as Thomsonfly.

4th | In Toronto, Floyd Patterson defeated challenger Tom McNeeley with a fourth-round knockout to retair world heavyweight boxing championship. Tom's son, Peter McNeeley, would become Mike Tyson's firs opponent upon the latter's release from prison in 1995. On the same evening, Sonny Liston knocked ou Albert Westphal in a Philadelphia bout. It was the last bout for both Patterson and Liston, until they fac each other in 1962 in Chicago, with the Liston taking the title from Patterson.

8th | Brothers Brian, Dennis and Carl Wilson, their cousin Mike Love, and friend Al Jardine, known as "The Pendletones", saw the release of their first recorded song, called "Surfin'" (with "Luau" on the "B"-side For the single, record distributor Russ Regen renamed the group, The Beach Boys, and their first song peaked at #75 on the Billboard Hot 100 chart.

10th | Operation Plowshare, the American experiment in using atomic weapons for peaceful purposes, began with Project Gnome, the underground explosion of a 3 kiloton atomic bomb near Carlsbad, New Mexic Although the test device was placed 1,200 feet below the surface in a cavern of rock salt, water within salt was vaporized by the blast and sent a geyser of radioactive steam 300 above the surface.

16th | The British medical journal The Lancet published a letter from Dr. W. G. McBride, an Australian obstetrician in the Sydney suburb of Hurstville, New South Wales, with the heading "Thalidomide and Congenital Abnormalities" The letter, which brought the link between thalidomide and birth defects to world's attention, began "Sir- Congenital abnormalities are present in approximately 1.5% of babies. In recent months, I have observed that the incidence of multiple severe abnormalities in babies deliverec women who were given the drug thalidomide ("Distaval") during pregnancy, as an anti-emitic or as a sedative, to be almost 20%..."

rd A crowded railroad car, carrying Christmas shoppers, as well as students and migrant workers heading home for the holiday, jumped a track near Catanzaro in Southern Italy, and plunged down a 100-foot embankment and into the rain swollen Fiumarella River, killing 71 people. The dead were from the villages of Cerrisi, Decollatura, and Soveria Mannelli. The engineer, Ciro Micelli, survived and was later sentenced to ten years in prison for manslaughter after a court found that he had taken the curved railroad track at almost twice the speed limit.

th The Maxwell House Hotel, at one time the most luxurious hotel in Nashville, and the inspiration for Maxwell House coffee, was completely destroyed by a fire on Christmas night. Although eight U.S. Presidents had stayed at the inn over the years, it later became a residential hotel.

th The Empire State Building, at that time still the tallest skyscraper in the world, was sold to a group of investors headed by Lawrence A. Wien for $65,000,000. In what was described, at that time, as "the most complex transaction in real estate history", the closing required the services of almost 100 professionals. It took place at the headquarters of the seller, the Prudential Insurance Company, in Newark, and the signing of the necessary documents took more than two hours.

th France's President, Charles de Gaulle, delivered his annual New Year's address on national television and radio, and announced that in the coming year, his listeners "would see the end of French Algeria 'one way or another'" and that with the withdrawal of French Army forces from Africa, 1962 would be "the year the army will be regrouped in Europe". The declaration was a shock to most of the one million French residents of north Africa who had still hoped that their homes would not become part of an Arab Muslim nation; Algeria would be granted its independence seven months later, on the 5th July.

th More than 25 years after it had been written, the Fourth Symphony of Dmitri Shostakovich was first performed. The Moscow Philharmonic Orchestra, conducted by Kirill Kondrashin, played the symphony at the Great Hall of the Moscow Conservatory. The original score had been destroyed during World War II, but was reconstructed from sources discovered in 1960.

st Ireland's first national television station, Telefís Éireann (later RTÉ), began broadcasting. A speech by Irish President Éamon de Valera opened the new era. Previously, the eastern area of the Republic of Ireland was able to receive broadcasts from the BBC from Great Britain.

PEOPLE IN POWER

Robert Menzies
1949-1966
Australia
Prime Minister

Charles de Gaulle
1959-1969
France
Président

Juscelino Kubitschek
1956-1961
Brazil
President

John Diefenbaker
1957-1963
Canada
Prime Minister

Mao Zedong
1943-1976
China
Government of China

Heinrich Lübke
1959-1969
Germany
President of Germany

Rajendra Prasad
1950-1962
India
1st President of India

Giovanni Gronchi
1955-1962
Italy
President

Hiroito
1926-1989
Japan
Emperor

Adolfo López Mateos
1958-1964
Mexico
President of Mexico

Nikita Khrushchev
1958-1964
Russia
Premier

Hendrik Verwoerd
1958-1966
South Africa
Prime Minister

John F. Kennedy
1961-1963
United States
President

Théo Lefèvre
1961-1965
Belgium
Prime Minister

Keith Holyoake
1960-1972
New Zealand
Prime Minister

Harold Macmillan
1957-1963
United Kingdom
Prime Minister

Tage Erlander
1946-1969
Sweden
Prime Minister

Viggo Kampmann
1960-1962
Denmark
Prime Minister

Francisco Franco
1936-1975
Spain
President

János Kádár
1961-1965
Hungary
Hungarian Working
People's Party

The Year You Were Born 1961
Book by Sapphire Publishing